Turn of the Century

Also by Nancy Smiler Levinson

CHRISTOPHER COLUMBUS
Voyager to the Unknown

I LIFT MY LAMP
Emma Lazarus and the Statue of Liberty

SWEET NOTES, SOUR NOTES

Turn

of the Century

OUR NATION
ONE HUNDRED
YEARS AGO

Nancy Smiler Levinson

LODESTAR BOOKS
Dutton ◆ New York

Acknowledgments

I wish to express my gratitude to Bruce J. Schulman, associate professor of history at Boston University, for his insightful suggestions during the preparation of my manuscript. I would also like to thank the following for their assistance during my research: the Beverly Hills Public Library staff; the state historical societies of Iowa and Nebraska; the office of U.S. Congressman Anthony Beilenson; the UCLA Oral History Project; the U.S. Labor Department; and the Labor Management Documentation Center, New York State School of Industrial Labor Relations, Cornell University; and the U.S. Patent Office.

I am ever grateful for the abiding support of my family, writing friends, and colleagues of the Society of Children's Book Writers and Illustrators, as well as for the good fortune of having as my editor Virginia Buckley, who continues to guide me with wisdom and thoughtfulness.

Copyright © 1994 by Nancy Smiler Levinson

Library of Congress Cataloging-in-Publication Data

Levinson, Nancy Smiler.
   Turn of the century: America one hundred years ago / Nancy Smiler Levinson.—1st ed.
     p. cm.
   Includes bibliographical references and index.
   ISBN 0-525-67433-0
   1. United States—History—1865-1900—Juvenile literature.
[1. United States—History—1865-1900.]   I. Title.
E661.L667   1994
973.8'9—dc20
                                                        93–4604
                                                         CIP
                                                         AC

Published in the United States by Lodestar Books,
an affiliate of Dutton Children's Books,
a division of Penguin Books USA Inc.,
375 Hudson Street, New York, New York 10014

Published simultaneously in Canada
by McClelland & Stewart, Toronto

Editor: Virginia Buckley   Designer: Richard Granald

Printed in the U.S.A.   First Edition
10 9 8 7 6 5 4 3 2 1

Contents

"What we shall some day become will grow inexorably out of what today we are; and what we are now, in its turn, comes out of what earlier Americans were—out of what they did and thought and dreamed and hoped for, out of their trials and their aspirations, out of their shining victories and their dark and tragic defeats."

Bruce Catton, historian
1958

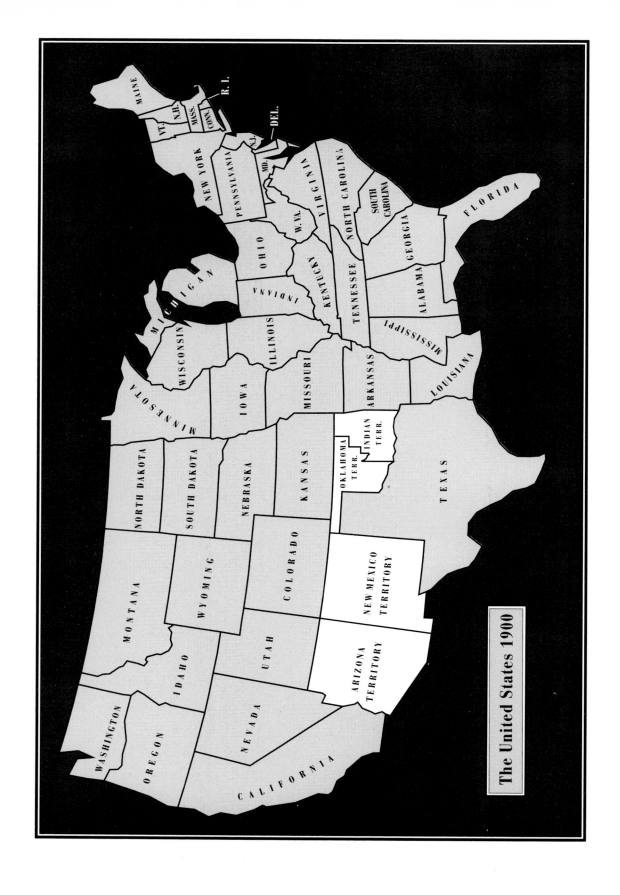

The United States 1900

1
Looking Back One Hundred Years

It was New Year's Eve 1899. In Los Angeles, California, at fifty cents per person, several parties boarded a special excursion train to ride to a Rubio Canyon resort for a social hop. In Boscobel, Wisconsin, families gathered at their church social halls to celebrate. In Washington, D.C., President and Mrs. William McKinley prepared for a White House reception to be held the following afternoon.

This was no ordinary New Year's Eve, however. The date marked the turn of a century. Although the century would not actually change until the period between 1900 and 1901, people everywhere felt that the start of 1900 was the time to mark the milestone event. As a boy living in New York City, Herbert Jaediker remembered "a lot of talk about what changes the new century would bring. The war with Spain was over and people looked forward to better times. For weeks, we kids collected pieces of wood for the New Year's Eve celebration on December 31. And what a celebration that was! Bonfires were lit in the middle of the streets and everyone was out throwing more wood, even furniture, on the fires to keep them going. The rich people held fancy balls, but the rest of us, even kids, blew horns in the streets. At twelve o'clock the boats on the river tooted their horns, and people banged pots and pans. It was the twentieth century!"

Even though it was an extraordinary occasion, New Year's Eve was not celebrated the way we are used to celebrating—with television specials, main street parades, and gala fireworks. Back in 1900, the country did not have the media technology it has today, and the times were different in many other respects as well.

Now, as we near the year 2000, not only are we approaching a new century—the twenty-first—we are also about to enter a new *millennium*. The span of a thousand years is far too much time for us to look back on. But when we view the era of a hundred years ago, we can see how much our nation has changed.

At the beginning of the nineteenth century, America was an agricultural nation, consisting of small, isolated communities scattered across the continental territories, with few roads and no communications networks. In comparatively short time, the agrarian nation began to grow into an urban and industrial society. By the end of the century the cities in the East had risen to great heights and were already suffering from overcrowding; and most of the land in the prairies and on the western frontier had been developed. The new frontier became machines, science, and technology. The era of individualism had dawned, and with the growth of capitalism, individuals seized every opportunity to pursue the American dream of wealth and power.

On the eve of 1900, America was hardly recognizable from the nation it had been only decades earlier. Americans could communicate across the land, if not by telephone everywhere, at least by telegraph or convenient mail delivery; they could travel by railroad to any designated place; and some lived and worked in buildings with electricity. Many Americans could afford the luxury of leisure time. And many were fighting for reforms to improve life and to ensure a continued

As capitalism grew, industrial finance came to be concentrated at the Stock Exchange in New York's Wall Street. New York Historical Society

democracy. With a population of 76 million, America was a young, developing nation, a model of self-government, a blessed land, that had grown rapidly with no interference from the outside world. But in the late 1890s, it would lose its innocence as it took its first awkward steps toward becoming a world power.

The story of America one hundred years ago is packed with events, names, dates, facts, and arguments. Like any study of history, this story is full of many interpretations, viewpoints, and questions, and it is forever open to further questioning. And like all studies of the past, it is foremost a story of turning points and of dramas large and small—the dramas of people and how they lived their lives.

2

The Iron Horse

One night in July 1881, fifteen-year-old Kate Shelley and her mother stood anxiously looking through a window of their Iowa farmhouse. Outside a raging storm was swelling the waters of Honey Creek, which emptied into the swiftly flowing Des Moines River.

They had already rescued the livestock from the flooded barn and moved the animals to higher ground, and they had calmed the frightened younger children in their beds. But the storm grew worse, and their worries heightened.

Nearby lay the tracks of the Chicago and Northwestern Railroad, where Kate's father, an Irish immigrant, had worked as a section foreman before he died in an accident on the job. About eleven o'clock, Kate and her mother heard an engine whistle. But no train was scheduled in either direction at that hour. Suddenly, they heard a crash and the hissing of steam. They knew at once what had happened.

The No. 11, an engine from the Moingona station, had been

sent ahead to check the track's safety for an express passenger train scheduled to pass through at midnight. The Honey Creek wooden bridge had been washed out, and the No. 11 had plunged into the river below.

The women were horrified. Kate knew she had to help the men and get word to the station operator to stop the midnight train. Quickly, she improvised a light by hanging a miner's lamp inside the frame of an old lantern and hurried out into the night. Climbing through the thick underbrush along a steep and slippery hillside, she reached the bridge. There she heard two men shouting for help and saw them desperately clinging to a tree.

All she could do was try to reach the Moingona station a mile away. Following the tracks, she came to the Des Moines River bridge, a long span with no handrail. Just as she started to cross it, her lantern flickered and went out. Only flashes of lightning helped guide her. Frantic, Kate began to make her way across the bridge timbers, crawling over railroad ties that were eighteen inches apart and studded with spikes. Rain and wind lashed at her, while below, there roared a furious flood. At last she reached the end of the bridge. Then dragging herself to her feet, she managed to run to the station, where she told the operator about the disaster. The survivors who had escaped were rescued (two other men aboard were killed), and a message was telegraphed to the midnight train, saving the lives of two hundred grateful people.

Kate was hailed a heroine and the dramatic event was recorded in the annals of America's railroad folklore. With the advent of steel rails and freight and passenger cars after the Civil War, and the later advancement of gasoline engines over steam power, the railroad changed America's way of life like no other invention or institution in the country's history. The great iron horse—streaking across the nation with wheels clacking on the silver rails, trailing puffs of smoke, its mournful whistle carried on the wind—became a symbol of power and progress, glamour and freedom. It transported people and their

Union Pacific's Overland Limited passing Pulpit Rock, Utah, near the Wyoming Border, 1900
Wyoming State Museum, Stimson Collection

products across stretches of wilderness, over deep rivers, and through passes of majestic mountain ranges. It was the biggest business in the United States, and it made possible nearly all other industry. People everywhere, especially poets and painters, romanticized the railroad. The names of the company lines rang out across the land— Chesapeake & Ohio; Denver and Rio Grande; the Atchison, Topeka, and the Santa Fe. The railroad stirred America's blood.

The Civil War had created new demands in the largely agricultural nation, and the railroads expanded to fill those demands. Not only did they transport troops, but booming industries grew in manufacturing and supplying those troops with arms and ammunition, boots, wool clothing and blankets, and preserved foods. After the war, the cattle industry flourished as refrigerator cars transported cattle to slaughterhouses and meat-packing plants. And to build railroads and keep them running, other big businesses rose to fill the need for timber, quarry stone, coal, iron and other ores, and most importantly, steel.

Although freight was carried back and forth between western markets and eastern seaports with increasing ease and rapidity, passengers had a rough time of it. A bride named Lizzie Miles rode all the way from Kansas to her new home in Superior, Montana, sitting in nothing but a "common boxcar, with homemade [lumber] seats of the sort used in an old schoolhouse." Some of the other riders even had to get out and help lift derailed cars back onto the tracks!

Another passenger who found train travel miserable was a young man named George Pullman. He had been a cabinetmaker and clerk in a country store, but business there was so dull that he went to the heartland city of Chicago to seek a money-making opportunity. And he met success. In 1867 he founded the Pullman Palace Car Company and devised and built hotel cars to provide passengers with every possible comfort. Soon, Pullman car interiors were luxuriously designed with cherry wood and plush upholstery and were lighted by oil lamps. The sleeper car came complete with washrooms and linen-dressed beds (the first passengers had to be politely asked to remove their boots before reclining on the linens), and the elaborately furnished dining car offered a bill of fare that included such dishes as mutton chops, quail on toast, and plum pudding. Enterprising George Pullman had indeed found his money-making opportunity.

Like many American businesses that have been built on a grand scale by ambitious achievers, the railroads certainly ranked among the greatest. But while it helped make the nation an industrial empire, the railroad industry did not always benefit the entire nation.

From the start, the U.S. federal government, eager for continued national growth, had spurred on construction. It gave the railroad corporations many millions of acres of prime farmland and rich

timberland and loaned them millions of dollars. Individual states also helped with land grants and loans. In order to clear the land for the railroads, the U.S. army brutally forced Native Americans from their lands, where their ancestors had lived for centuries. In time, continued corrupt practices by railroad leaders led Congress to set guidelines and enact regulations against fraud and monopolistic control, but by then the leaders had filled their pockets with profits beyond any ever imagined.

The men who built the railroads were fierce and competitive. They cheated one another, swindled the public, and exploited their employees, paying workers pitifully low wages. Sometimes, they com-

Cornelius Vanderbilt
Library of Congress

bined companies to eliminate competition, or they offered bargain rates to certain shippers only to win their freight business. A favored method for making money dishonestly was to issue stocks and shares beyond the true value of the business, which enabled companies to raise money from investors while giving them little or no return for their money. This was known as "watered stock," a term from early cattle-drive days when cattle were kept thirsty until shortly before arriving at market, then fed salt and allowed to drink vast quantities of water so they would look fatter and beefier than they really were.

These men came to be called robber barons. Among the first was the unschooled and tart-tongued Cornelius Vanderbilt, who had grown up in a poor Dutch family of nine children on Staten Island in New York State. His father was a ferryman, and young Cornelius tried to talk him into expanding the business. When the elder Vanderbilt refused, in 1810 Cornelius, then sixteen, borrowed one hundred dollars from his mother, bought an old barge, and started his own ferry service—competing against his father for business. The following year, "Commodore" Cornelius Vanderbilt, as he was called, developed a fleet of steamboat carriers, ferrying freight and passengers between Staten Island and New York City, and later serving the east coast down to South Carolina.

During the Civil War, he abandoned his fleet for the more lucrative business of train transportation and eventually bought the New York Central line. A decade later, he had multiplied his fortune many times over. He had voted himself a bonus of 20 million dollars in watered stock and an additional 6 million in cash! By then, he came up against his biggest rival—the Erie Railroad, which was controlled by a trio of robber barons: Daniel Drew, James Fisk, and Jay Gould. Vanderbilt tried to buy them out, but they kept issuing more worthless stock and raising more money until Vanderbilt finally admitted defeat for the first time. "It never pays to kick a skunk," he said. By the end of that financial war, there were so many swindled Erie Railroad stockholders that the company's reputation collapsed in ruin. As for Vanderbilt, he died one of the richest men in America.

Meanwhile, far out West in California, four other men had met and sealed a partnership: Leland Stanford, a grocer; Charles Crocker, who ran a dry goods clothing store; Mark Hopkins, a bookkeeper; and Collis P. Huntington, who had ventured from Connecticut during the gold rush and had begun his hardware business career as a peddler. They were fulfilling the dream of a fifth acquaintance, who had dreamed of building a railroad across the Sierra Nevada mountains from California to connect with the rest of the country. But he had died of yellow fever. The foursome won a government contract to build the first western portion of the railroad—the Central Pacific. Thousands of laborers, mostly Chinese recruited from their homeland as well as from scattered California mining towns, battered their way through mountains and over perilous steep grades. They were paid a pittance in wages, and they toiled under blistering sun and against blinding blizzards and avalanches until the enormous task was done.

Finally, one spring day in 1869, a momentous event took place.

Chinese laborers building the Central Pacific Railway, which was to be joined with the Union Pacific, completing the country's first transcontinental railroad. Here at Secrettown Trestle in northern California, laborers toiled with picks and shovels, chisels and hammers, black powder, wheelbarrows, and one-horse dump carts. Southern Pacific Photo Association of American Railroads

The Central Pacific of the West was joined with the Union Pacific, the government-owned railroad line of the East. The occasion happened at a spot called Promontory Point, Utah. The great news of the first transcontinental railroad was tapped across the "talking wires" of the telegraph to every city, cow town, and whistle-stop. Farm and factory, country and city came together. The nation had truly become one.

People arrived by the millions to lay claim to western acres and to the Great Plains, the area that reached from the Mississippi Valley

Broadside advertising land with reasonable financing to attract a new immigrant population State Historical Society of Iowa

to the Rocky Mountains and from the Canadian border to Texas. And the railroads brought them there. Earlier pioneers from the eastern states and from Europe had already begun settling the fertile prairies and lush pastures of the American plains. They were the ranching and farming homesteaders, who had come after the swarm of gold and silver miners. But mid-century, most newcomers were European immigrants, encouraged by the government and the steamship and railroad corporations to come live and work in "the gardens of the West."

Transporting millions of people across the country was a big business. A better future was for sale, and the best way to sell it was by advertising. The Northern Pacific railroad line advertised a speedy journey to acres of "the finest farming land at the lowest prices ever offered by any railroad company." The Illinois Central declared that on their lands people would find "the blessings of civilization." Oklahoma offered large quantities of copper and lead. Immigrants were promised everything from free homes or easy-purchase credit to temperate climate, large crops every year, and bountiful hunting for deer, bear, antelope, and buffalo.

Agents were sent abroad, competing with one another to sign up the most people to bring back to their states. One agent for Nebraska, Mr. C. B. Neilson, wrote home from Denmark: "The battle is won for our state, but it was a hard fought battle. . . . The fall emigration to Nebraska of people with sufficient capital to commence work on our prairie will be very large. On Monday I go to Sweden and Norway and will have easy work there. I shall try my best to beat the agent for Minnesota. . . ."

Immigrants were eager to leave famine, overpopulation, and political and religious injustice to come to America. Although they found hope on the prairies, they also suffered greatly. They faced hot, dry winds and dust storms, blizzards and bitter cold, drought, fire, disease, desperate loneliness, and infestation of billions of grasshoppers that devoured every inch of crop while farmers stood helplessly by. Many people went mad or died. Only the strongest could endure, and those who did showed a remarkable ability to survive.

At mid-century, two brothers, Henrik and Osten Boe (Bö), came to Minnesota from their hamlet in Norway. Henrik settled in Northfield and prospered as a hardware merchant. Osten longed for a spread of land, a symbol of dignity and stability, and he found it in the remote township of Aastad. For his new wife, Caroline, and growing family, Osten built a one-room sod house, a home made of earth. Ten years later, when lumber became more available, he built a log cabin. He and Caroline had nine children. Two died in infancy, and two died of diptheria, choking to death in their parents' arms. Yet Osten and Caroline continued to count the blessings that God had granted them.

On the farm, Osten first raised wheat, and as he increased his acreage he added barley, oats, rye, clover, flax, and potatoes. He worked long, tedious days and also was carpenter, cobbler, hunter, and fisherman. Caroline provided meals for the family, spun yarn, wove cloth, sewed and patched, made rugs and bedding, tended the orchard, put up preserves and dried fruit, and made candles and soap. Always they struggled in the face of one natural disaster after another. Once, in the midst of a raging snowstorm, Osten made his way to the barn to milk the cows, tying a rope from the house to the barn so he could retrace his steps. The blizzard was so blinding and the wind so ferocious that he could not make it back from the barn. He remained trapped inside for three days.

While the great iron horse led so many to the land of hope and promise, it also was a major reason for the displacement and destruction of Native Americans. White men felt entitled to build railroads farther and farther into native territory, unconcerned that they were disrupting and threatening Indians' unique culture and way of life. At first, whites met with tribes peacefully, offering promises of payment and fair treatment in exchange for land. Many tribes, swept along by these strange, new events, accepted the offers, only to find that they had been tricked into signing away their homeland and hunting grounds and were slowly being isolated onto remote reservations.

Native Americans fought for their land, their lives, their very souls. After so many broken promises on the part of the white men, so much trampling of their native lands, and the slaughter of millions of buffalo, which provided them with food and shelter, there were uprisings and massacres. U.S. army units were dispatched to fight Indian revolts, and killings on both sides were brutal. Little by little, the settlers triumphed, as the military rounded up one tribe after another and confined them to faraway places, where many starved to death.

By the end of the nineteenth century, the golden age of railroads had made America immensely wealthy. And the nation had

Cheyenne Buck. **Painting by Frederic Remington**
The National Cowboy Hall of Fame, Oklahoma City

become "smaller," because the railroad had so greatly reduced travel time; a journey by train from New York to San Francisco, once a six-month ordeal, now took only six days. In 1900, Americans were using nearly two hundred thousand miles of track. Railroad companies no longer competed with one another as viciously as before, and the lines were serving the nation's newest demands—especially for ever-rising modern cities—by continually supplying more raw materials, manufactured goods and machinery, and farmers' produce. Seventy-nine billion tons of freight were hauled every year, seven times more than the amount transported at the end of the Civil War. The railroad was

◆ *Massacre at Wounded Knee* ◆

For decades, Native Americans had suffered loss of life, land, cultural values, and tradition. By 1890, most had been confined to reservations. They were starving and feared the total extinction of their people. But that fall, the Sioux living in South Dakota suddenly found renewed hope for survival. They embraced a new religious movement, which came to them from a Paiute Indian prophet who envisioned a new era of good fortune. It was called the Ghost Dance Religion, and it promised the return of their dead and the disappearance of white men from their land if they engaged in sacred ghost dancing and chanting. Desperate, the Sioux began days and nights of frenzied dancing.

By December, government agents at the Pine Ridge Reservation began to fear a Sioux uprising, so they arranged for police to put a stop to the ceremonies. They also ordered the arrest of Chief Sitting Bull at nearby Standing Rock Reservation. But Sitting Bull resisted, and friends tried to protect him. A scuffle took place outside his cabin, and the great warrior and leader was shot to death. Tribes people panicked and fled. Soldiers went after them and by nightfall rounded up some 350, with the intention of returning them to their reservations. That night, they all stayed at an army campsite called Wounded Knee, as soldiers stood watch. In the morning, the captured were ordered to give up their arms before setting out on the trip back. Historians are unsure of exactly what happened next, but one version of the incident recalled that a young deaf Indian refused, and when someone tried to grab his rifle, it went off. Soldiers took the shot as a signal that they were being attacked, and they began shooting wildly. Within minutes, the site at Wounded Knee had become a scene of slaughter. Some three hundred Native American men, women, and children lay dead. Twenty-five soldiers also died. They were buried later with military honors, but the bodies of the Indians were left on the frozen ground because of an approaching blizzard. During the following January, they were dug up and buried in a common unmarked grave.

also the nation's biggest employer, with well over a million workers at the turn of the century, whose average annual salary was $567. It was also a chief cause of accidents and deaths, which resulted from collapsing bridges, boiler blowups, and blizzards, to animals on the track, runaway trains, and spectacular collisions.

Back in Cayce, Kentucky, there was a boy named John Luther Jones, who, like many boys then, had taken the locomotive to heart. He started out on the Mobile and Ohio line as a fireman, stoking the locomotive, and later became a freight and passenger engineer on the Illinois Central. One April night in 1900, he and his fireman, Sim Webb, were asked to take out the speedy Cannonball from Memphis down to Canton, Mississippi. They were late in getting started, so Jones ran at full throttle to make up time on a mail schedule. But early the next morning, only miles from Canton, a freight train ahead was stalled on the track, and the block signals on the line weren't working. The Cannonball couldn't be stopped in time. Jones told Sim Webb to jump to safety, which he did. And the brave engineer stayed with his engine, trying to slow it down. The locomotive rammed into the freight car, but with less force than it would have if Jones had bailed out, too, and all the passengers' lives were spared. Jones's body was found in the wreckage with one hand on the throttle and the other on the air-brake lever. The engineer, who was called Casey Jones—referring to his hometown of Cayce—has lived on in legend, one of railroad folklore's most popular heroes.

3

Inventions, Inventions, Inventions

$\mathbf{F}$or years, a poor, struggling inventor from Philadelphia named Charles Goodyear had been fascinated with rubber, a product that came from a milky fluid found in certain South American trees. Rubber was durable and elastic, showing promise for many uses, especially for making boots, but it was unusable in its natural form because it cracked in cold temperatures and disintegrated under the sun.

After much trial and error in trying to stabilize the material, one day in a workshop in New York, Goodyear spilled a gummy mixture of rubber and sulfur on a hot stove. To his amazement he found the solution to the problem! The heat had scientifically "cured" the rubber compound, making it both elastic and durable. Goodyear had discovered the process of vulcanizing rubber, a revolutionary find. By the end of the century, Goodyear's invention was most notably used for pneumatic tires, a boon to the newly growing automobile industry.

Rubber became one of America's most valuable inventions. But it was just one of thousands of inventions that expressed Americans' fascination with technology and with finding ways for self-improvement. America was becoming known as a "nation of tinkerers."

Since the early nineteenth century, people with the pioneer spirit had found means to live on treeless plains, to supply water to arid country, and to turn raw materials into finished industrial products. In time, they came to invent the telegraph, the steam tractor, cables for electric streetcars, and machines to manufacture shoes and carpeting. They invented compressed air brakes to help bring locomotives to a speedy halt, making railroad travel safer than ever before. They invented the safety pin, the safety razor, and the safety lock. One tinkerer came up with the idea for a zipper and another with the idea for an apple parer. A mid-century patent commissioner proclaimed, "We are an inventive people. Our merchants invent, our soldiers and sailors invent, our professional men invent, aye, our women and school children invent." Between 1860 and 1890, U.S. patents were issued for 440,000 inventions.

No single inventor transformed as many lives as did the extraordinary genius Thomas Alva Edison, who held a total of 1,093 patents. His electric light bulb, created in 1879 after nine years of work, became the symbol of American invention. When he developed an entire electrical generating and distributing system, he emerged as architect of the electric revolution. Among his other inventions were the stock ticker, the phonograph, and, with able assistance, the motion picture camera and projector.

Edison was born in Milan, Ohio, in 1847. When he was seven, his family moved to Port Huron, Michigan, where Edison started school. His persistent questioning and dreaminess annoyed his strict teacher so much that he was berated for disruptive behavior. The teacher thought he was a dunce and called him addled. Edison's mother took him out of school and began instructing him at home. (He briefly attended another school a few years later.) At home, chemistry especially intrigued him, and he set about experimenting in his basement, marking his bottles of chemicals "Poison" to keep people away from his laboratory. When he was twelve, he went to work as a "news butcher" on the railroad, selling newspapers, tobacco, and candy to passengers on the Grand Trunk Railway during the four-hour ride between Port Huron and Detroit. In Detroit, he spent afternoons reading in the public library before catching the train back. In an empty corner of a baggage car, Edison set up a second chemistry laboratory, but one day an experiment burst into flame and started a small fire. The conductor put out the fire just in time and threw all the boy's equipment off the train.

Later, Edison learned telegraphy and worked as a telegraph operator, roaming from city to city. In Boston, he turned his full attention to inventing. Soon he opened a workshop in Newark, New Jersey, and then moved to Menlo Park, another town in New Jersey, where he became known as a wizard, whose greatest pleasure and challenge was his constant work.

One of the inventions for which he had been given a patent was a motion picture camera. Adding photographic devices produced by other inventors, Edison set up a film studio and developed a mechanism that projected images onto a screen. On an April evening in 1896, a crowd gathered at a New York City music hall to see something new and curious—a motion picture. The audience watched in amazement as pictures of two girls dancing an "umbrella dance," a comic boxing bout, and a scene of ocean waves breaking on a coastline flickered across the screen. Newspaper reports said that the ocean seemed so realistic that people in the front rows flinched for fear they might get wet. The *New York Times* called the motion picture "all wonderfully real and singularly exhilarating." It was the last decade of the century, and the beginning of a new era of amusement at the movies.

For some years, a man who taught the deaf and was particularly interested in speech patterns and the nature of sound had realized that

Thomas Edison working on the first motion picture projector in his laboratory in West Orange, New Jersey
U.S. National Archives

the human voice could be transmitted electrically. His name was Alexander Graham Bell (he was born the same year as Edison). He and his assistant, Thomas A. Watson, worked on an instrument to send spoken words in a Boston electrical shop. In 1875, they first managed to get feeble voice sounds to pass through a wire, but failed to make words understandable. Then one day the following year, from two different rented rooms in the same boardinghouse, they succeeded in communicating two complete sentences. The assistant heard Bell say, "Mr. Watson, please come here. I want you." This was a momentous occasion.

Bell's telephone caught on quickly. It was an easy machine to use and required no special technical knowledge. When Bell established his telephone company, six hundred local subscribers—mostly businesses—eagerly signed up even though each private line was connected to only a few other points, messages often had to be repeated,

Alexander Graham Bell demonstrating long distance telephone transmission over the first New York to Chicago line in 1892
Library of Congress

and rates were high ($150 per year for a business). By the turn of the century, 677,000 telephones were in use, connected by a million miles of telephone wire.

Long distance communication was not confined solely to the transmission of signals through wires, however. Wireless telegraphy was developed by a German, Heinrich Hertz, and an Italian, Guglielmo Marconi, who showed the world that signals could be transmitted through the air. This helped lead the way for the birth of radio.

During much of the nineteenth century, there was little work acceptable for women trying to earn a decent living. All that was considered respectable was teaching, working in a library or as a clerk in a store, or serving as a governess to children in a wealthy home. Most working women were exploited by the drudgery of factory or farm work. Then one man, known as "the great grandfather of office machinery," made it possible for thousands of women to work at "genteel jobs" in offices across the country.

Christopher L. Sholes was a dreamy sort of man, who earned a living as a customs collector in Milwaukee, Wisconsin. He also liked to tell stories, recite poetry, play chess, and tinker with machines. One of his persistent dreams was to invent a machine that would print words directly onto paper, a sort of practical writing machine—a typewriter. But with every attempt to build such a complex instrument full of tiny levers and shafts and wheels, he ran into a different problem. And besides, Sholes didn't know how to go about adapting his machine to mass production. At last, he took a model to Thomas Edison in his New Jersey laboratory, and Edison offered the final advice that Sholes needed to perfect it. Eventually, the Remington Arms Company bought the rights to the typewriter, although it didn't sell well right away. When it caught on, however, beginning around 1895, it helped to spur a social revolution.

Another kind of communication revolution had already begun when a German immigrant, Ottmar Mergenthaler, working in a cousin's machine shop in Washington, D.C., devised a multi-operational machine that produced printing type. This was the linotype machine. With this and the development of printing plates and the rotary press, newspapers, books, and magazines could be printed not just one page at a time but by the thousands! Speedy, mass printing spread knowledge and brought people throughout the world closer together.

Farm production had been revolutionized early in the century with the invention of the horse-drawn reaper by a young Virginia farmer named Cyrus McCormick. With some assistance, he built a model that cut and collected wheat, and when it was publicly demonstrated, he showed how it did the work of six laborers with a hand tool. The McCormick reaper was neither the first nor the best, but it came along at a time when farmers needed a way to harvest large wheat crops. McCormick had a good head for business, too, and by the century's end, his manufacturing company took the lead with vastly improved and updated machinery.

The research spirit was high as men and women made important medical and scientific advances that contributed to human welfare. In the late 1890s, combined American and European efforts helped to understand and conquer mosquito-caused malaria. Scientists were discovering immunization against epidemic diseases such as diptheria, as well as anesthesia—notably novocaine—so that surgery and dental work could be performed without a patient suffering pain. Experiments were under way to gain knowledge about the effects of unclean water and vitamin-deficient diets. And in 1896, Edison invented a flouroscope, an instrument for viewing X-ray images on the newly invented X-ray machine.

The railroads had long made one kind of travel possible, but now there were new methods of transporation. In 1888, the first electric traction streetcar system was installed in Richmond, Viriginia, and nine years later Boston boasted the first subway. People could even be lifted to the tops of ever-rising skyscrapers by way of an Elisha G. Otis invention—the elevator.

At a banquet meeting of the Association of the Edison Illuminating Company in New York in 1897, two gentlemen met for the first time. One was Thomas Edison, and the other was a young employee of the company named Henry Ford, who had grown up on a Michigan farm and left for Detroit to work as a machinist. There, he began experimenting with gasoline engines, and before long he had built a model automobile with a steering tiller, bicycle wheels, and an engine from the exhaust pipe of a steam engine. In time, many came to call the auto a horseless carriage, but those who believed the new-fangled invention was nothing but a danger on the road called it a "devil's wagon." In 1900, Vermont passed a law requiring a driver to

Henry Ford in his first motor car, powered by a two-cylinder, four-cycle gasoline motor
From the collection of Henry Ford Museum and Greenfield Village

have someone on foot or on horseback carry a red warning flag one-eighth of a mile ahead of the vehicle.

No single person is credited with inventing the automobile. There were many pioneers in both America and Europe. But Henry Ford eventually built one of the world's largest industrial corporations. Ford was an admirer of the great inventor Edison. At the association banquet in New York, Ford told the older man about his automotive dream. "Young man, you have it—the self-contained unit carrying its own fuel," Edison replied. "Keep at it!"

In Dayton, Ohio, two brothers were deeply occupied in their bicycle shop. They were building a double-winged glider, which they continued developing until they believed it large enough to lift a man. At that point, Wilbur and Orville Wright needed more space and better weather conditions, so in the winter of 1899 they journeyed to

Kitty Hawk, North Carolina, where they began their first glider test flights. They had high hopes for their invention.

As the new century approached and technology was revolutionizing the country beyond anything ever envisioned, many people found themselves remembering something a patent commissioner had said decades earlier. He had declared that so many "advancements made for human improvement" already existed that it was impossible to believe any more could come along. The commissioner was certain that all possible inventions had been invented.

4

The Robber Barons

On a farm in upstate New York there was a boy who, like most boys around the village, fished, swam, skated, plodded off to school with his books slung over his shoulder, and dutifully attended his farming chores. He was John D. Rockefeller, son of a peddler father and strict Baptist mother, and when he milked the cows and pulled weeds his parents paid him small sums. Every penny he hid away in a china bowl. Once, when he was twelve, he dug potatoes for a neighbor, and the thirty-seven and a half cents he earned for a day's work went into the china bowl too. But that time a new idea occurred to him. His father had engaged him in shrewd bargaining deals to teach him how to be sharp and alert, and John suddenly realized that the same amount of money could be made in an easier way and not require a full day's work. It could be earned by charging interest on a loan. John understood that money itself could make money. The boy learned his lessons well, and he seemed to make up his mind early in life that he wanted to acquire great wealth.

When John was fourteen, his family moved to Cleveland,

John D. Rockefeller
Library of Congress

Ohio, where he continued his high school education. He went on to study bookkeeping at a business school for a few months, and then at sixteen he set off to make his fortune. His first job was working as an assistant bookkeeper for a small company that shipped fruits and vegetables. The year was 1855, and his annual salary was three hundred dollars.

Rockefeller's big opportunity came some years later at Oil Creek, Pennsylvania. Oil had been discovered there, after the first well in the United States had been drilled elsewhere in that state. At that time, petroleum was coming into demand for use in illuminating kerosene lamps and lubricating machines; by early in the next century, however, oil would become the world's most valued and sought-after product. Rockefeller was sent by a group of businessmen to investigate Oil Creek's future. The area did indeed look promising to Rockefeller, but he reported back that it had "no future." Then, behind the men's backs he invested his own savings in the new refineries.

That was the beginning of Rockefeller's rise to becoming the king of oil, controller of the world's largest monopoly of the time, the Standard Oil Company. John D. Rockefeller, who had once thought about ways to make money that were easier than a day's toil, began to live for his work. It was said that throughout his life he rarely missed a day on the job.

During his climb he acquired more and more power, but it never seemed to be enough. He always set his sights on gaining yet greater power, and the best way to do that was to get rid of the competition whenever other oil-producing companies sprang up. One of the methods he used to squeeze them out was by making secret deals with railroad companies, convincing them to lower their shipping rates for him in exchange for his freight business. As the oil-producing industry grew, so did the need for faster and better transport of oil. Soon, a vast system of pipelines was built. Rockefeller took control of the pipelines and the distribution companies too. Certainly, he used unfair practices to continue his monopoly and prevent fair business competition. To ensure that the government didn't interfere, he even bribed many a legislator.

Another method to evade anti-monopoly laws was to buy out a competing company, allowing it to remain under its original ownership but holding its stocks in trusteeship under the Standard Oil Company's name. This way, in secrecy or not, the Rockefeller organization could still control all of its acquired corporations. Rockefeller and his staff had created something new in the business world. It was called a *trust*—a device for combining businesses, or a company whose foremost business was to own other companies all run by a single board of directors.

The Standard Oil Company set a pattern, and many corporations formed trusts that controlled industries such as steel, copper, tobacco, sugar, meat packing, rubber, leather, and farm machinery. By the 1890s, about five thousand companies had been consolidated into three hundred trusts—although by then the term *trust* held a different meaning and generally referred to big businesses of any kind. The American public became outraged, but the giant corporations could not be stopped. One government attempt was the Sherman Antitrust Act of 1890, which outlawed trusts, but this law was difficult to enforce and the big-business leaders found ways to get around it.

Although Rockefeller rose to his position by frequent wrongdoings, he also made unique contributions toward more efficient economic practices, as did other big businessmen who followed. Rockefeller introduced many innovations, such as modern cost accounting and a strategy of "vertical integration"—the process of combining all elements of production—from raw material extraction to sales and distribution.

By setting the scene for the age of enterprise, Rockefeller and Standard Oil helped to shape a new era of financial capitalism. With an enormous labor supply, new technology, and new ways to raise money to start and expand businesses, industry thrived, especially in northeastern cities. Business empires grew in an atmosphere that encouraged an economic theory of laissez-faire—a belief that for the good of the nation the individual should freely pursue his own economic interests without government interference or restrictions.

Many people, though, believed that the individual pioneer spirit was being carried far beyond proper bounds to selfishness, greed, and vulgarity. Rockefeller and other shrewd and unscrupulous men like him, who were consumed with ambition to gain power and make millions, came to be called robber barons. Even though the country had an elected government, America was really governed by a plutocracy—rule by the wealthy class. Writer Mark Twain and a literary friend, Charles Dudley Warner, wrote a novel satirizing business and political leaders. They created exaggerated, outrageous characters as symbols of the politicians and the get-rich-quick robber barons. They called the book *The Gilded Age*, which became the popular phrase to describe the era.

Some of the millionaires had grown up in wealthy families and

Andrew Carnegie
Library of Congress

were educated, while a handful of others had rags-to-riches stories to tell about their lives, like the fictional characters portrayed in popular books for children written by Horatio Alger, Jr. The Alger series, with such titles as *Ragged Dick* and *Luck and Pluck*, were about poor but honest lads—a shoe-shine boy, a newsboy, or a match boy—struggling against the pitfalls of life in the city jungle and triumphing in the end.

One of those extraordinary real-life rags-to-riches stories belonged to a man named Andrew Carnegie, who came from a poor family in Scotland. When Andrew was thirteen the Carnegies sailed to the United States to join relatives in Allegheny, Pennsylvania. Andrew's mother took in work at home binding shoes, and his father found a job in a cotton textile factory, where Andrew was also hired—as a bobbin boy. There, he worked in a dark, damp cellar twelve hours a day for $1.50 a week. Later, he went to work as a telegraph messenger boy in nearby Pittsburgh, quickly learning to send and decode messages well enough to become an operator. As a telegraph worker he met some of the city's most influential men, and he made it his business to get to know them so that in the future he would have helpful contacts.

By the time he was a young man, Carnegie had risen to a supervisory position at the western division of the Pennsylvania Railroad and had learned how to invest his money wisely. He made a fortune when he and some associates bought a farm on which oil had been found, and its worth rose at an astonishing rate. With oil and railroad profits, Carnegie invested heavily in iron. But he soon observed that the days of iron were nearing an end because something else was taking its place—steel.

Steel, an alloy or mixture, of one of earth's elements—iron ore —along with small amounts of other materials, became the mainstay of the modern industrial world after an Englishman and an American independently discovered a process to manufacture it. The method involved blasting cold air through cast iron (also called pig iron) in its glowing molten mass state, which made it even hotter. When oxygen from that air combined with the iron's carbon, the carbon was driven out. What remained was steel. Soon, this smelting process was refined, and it was possible for a single furnace to produce as much as one hundred tons of steel every twelve hours. Demands for its use were great—especially for railroads, bridges, ships, and the frameworks of newly rising skyscrapers.

In 1872, Carnegie observed the steel-making process and knew at once that "steel is king!" He bought and expanded production mills in Pennsylvania's sprawling Monongahela Valley and soon realized the advantage of owning not only the main raw material source—the iron ore—but also the equipment for steel production, the necessary transportation, and the manufacturing outlets. In the spirit of progress and individualism, he set out to do just that. But along the way to the top of his steel dynasty, he exploited and crushed other hardworking individuals trying to exercise their right to compete. He stopped at nothing to prevent competition, forcing other companies to choose

J. P. Morgan
Library of Congress

between selling to him on his terms or facing ruin. He also stopped at nothing to make sure that government officials passed laws favoring the industrial kings.

One robber baron who grew up wealthy and educated was a Wall Street banker named John Pierpont Morgan. He was born in Hartford, Connecticut, and schooled in Germany. It is said he was so intimidating that even his partners tiptoed in his presence. J. P. Morgan got his start as a banker and lawyer in his father's international banking firm, which had its headquarters in London. In time, J. P. came to wield so much power in his established banking firm, the House of Morgan, that once when the U.S. treasury's gold reserve was in trouble, the federal government went to him for a 62-million-dollar bailout. He and his colleagues sold that amount of gold to the government in return for bonds, which they cashed in as soon as their value rose. During another financial crisis, Morgan loaned vast amounts of money to several banks to keep them from closing. In

Upper Fifth Avenue
mansions, New York City
Library of Congress

1901, J. P. Morgan formed the first billion-dollar company, a combination of companies, including a merger with Carnegie Steel holdings, which became the United States Steel Corporation.

Robber barons lived lavishly. Cornelius Vanderbilt constructed a mansion the length of an entire block on Fifth Avenue in New York City and then built another in Newport, Rhode Island, which he called a cottage. Andrew Carnegie built a castle in Scotland and hired seventy-six servants to run it. He admitted that "there is no palace or great mansion in Europe with half the conveniences and scientific appliances which characterize the best mansions" in the United States, meaning telephones connecting the house to the stables and the gardener's quarters, steam pipes to carry heated air to every room, and electricity for light and "for calling a messenger."

One New York City millionaire, William Astor, declared that becoming a millionaire was in itself a "distinct profession." Astor, whose family amassed a fortune in real estate, and his wife produced a Social Register—a listing of four hundred names whom they considered to be the city's elite. The rich who were left out felt snubbed and humiliated. Mrs. Astor's ballroom was large enough to hold the same number of guests as the names on her social list—four hundred. Entertainment among the elite was often excessive. Balls and dinners, where champagne and diamond tiaras were commonplace, cost thousands of dollars to arrange. At one dinner, hundreds of white doves were released to fly among the guests. At other affairs, guests discovered black pearls in their oysters, or ladies found a gold bracelet when they unrolled their napkins. Mrs. Stuyvesant Fish hosted a dinner in honor of her pet monkey, which she dressed in formal attire. In 1897, when an average salary was about five hundred dollars a year, and many families could barely survive on this low amount, one hostess who was criticized for giving a particularly costly affair announced that she did it to "help stimulate business."

Travel abroad was popular among the wealthy, who frequently sailed with their servants and nannies to look after their children. Wealthy travelers often took as many as twenty trunks with them. In Europe, they snatched up art treasures, statuary, and rare tapestries to ship home to impress their friends.

Rockefeller, Carnegie, and Morgan all lived well into the twentieth century. Despite their decades of ruthless business dealings, all became known as generous philanthropists. Rockefeller, raised by his mother in the Baptist tradition, donated millions of dollars to form a foundation to aid medical research, education, and other social institutions. Carnegie, who believed that a worthy Christian citizen should devote half of one's life to making money and the other half to giving it away for good use, left his money to schools, libraries, and scientific laboratories. He also built eight thousand church organs. Morgan, an Episcopalian, contributed large sums to educational and medical causes, as well as for building a cathedral in New York City.

The rise of the robber barons and their industrial kingdoms was indeed remarkable. Their combined wealth and power reached the greatest heights as the new century dawned.

5

Workers, Unite!

Every morning at 7:30, young Pauline Newman began her job at the Triangle Shirtwaist Company near Washington Square Park in New York City. There on the ninth floor in a gloomy room, cold and damp in the winter and stifling in the summer, she trimmed threads from shirts when the operators were finished stitching. She and the other employees worked seven days a week until as late as nine in the evening during the busy season for a few dollars' wage, with no overtime pay or supper money—except for the reward of a little apple pie. To avoid drinking unclean water from the hall tap when they were thirsty, employees had to pay a precious two cents of their own to a pop bottle vendor who came around in hot weather.

The workers were watched by the management at every turn —when they arrived, went to the toilet, talked, or made an error, and when they didn't work fast enough. If the managers were displeased they would fine the women and deduct the amount from their weekly pay. Every Saturday, Pauline was reminded that if she didn't come to work on Sunday, she need not come back on Monday. Pauline couldn't allow that to happen. She lived with her mother and sisters in a two-room tenement, and they needed every cent they could get for food and rent.

In the Pennsylvania coal mining town of Bitumen, a twelve-year-old boy named Wyndham Mortimer joined his father and two brothers at work in the mines. The family lived in a shack nearby and was forced to buy everything from a store owned and operated by the mining bosses. The bosses also made the miners pay for their own dynamite and lamp oil, subtracted fifty cents a month for medical and blacksmith services, and wouldn't allow them to order anything from a mail-order catalog because the company controlled the local post office station too.

After several years confined to work in the dark, grimy caverns, in air thick with coal dust and lamp smoke, alongside scores of mules, Wyndham was found to be sickly and underweight. Despite the family's debts and their need for Wyndham's meager contribution, he was sent to live with a relative, where proper food and several months of sunlight helped restore his health. Back home again, he had no choice but to return to the mines.

Then one snowy Sunday at church, a farmer friend offered to sell Wyndham's father a portion of a freshly killed steer at a good price. Because buying outside of the company store was forbidden, Wyndham's father told the farmer to bring the side of beef in the middle of the night, which the man quietly did on a sled. But they were found out, and the whole family was fired. They were forced to move to another mining town, a move made even more difficult by the misery of a bitter winter.

Following that, Wyndham held a succession of jobs—alternating day and night shifts in a steel mill for twelve-hour periods, farming, and driving a team of horses hauling paving stones for a dollar a day—anything that came his way. Later in his life, he became a union leader, uniting workers exploited by their bosses so that they could fight for fair working conditions.

George Pullman, the hotel car magnate, had been praised for hiring more freed slaves than had any other industry leader. The men were hired as Pullman train porters to serve and assist passengers in the luxury railroad cars. For them, the work meant a chance to have a job and a home, and to be able to raise a family. At first, the porters were glad to accept Pullman's rigid rules of conduct and appearance: to smile at all times and greet each passenger, to make certain their uniforms were in perfect order, to follow precise instructions for folding linens and stacking laundry. In time, though, these rules became burdensome. The porters were made to work exceptionally long hours on the job with barely any time to themselves between train runs, and they had to pay for soiled or missing items, as well as for their own equipment, such as the shoe polish they used to shine the passengers' shoes. They also had to endure insensitive remarks and humiliating treatment before receiving a small tip, which they needed because they were the lowest paid group of railroad employees. Anyone who stood up for himself and his dignity was fired.

Pullman had built a company town outside Chicago, which housed thousands of his employees. There, he could completely control their lives by forcing them to shop in his stores, attend his schools, and worship in his churches—all at costs and rents that he dictated. Most of the costs were deducted from the workers' paychecks; once, a man was reportedly left with only seven cents at the end of a month. None of the black train porters were residents, however, because Pullman allowed only white families to live in his town. Neither did the newly growing labor groups in the 1890s allow blacks to join, so eventually black porters formed their own organization—the Brotherhood of Sleeping Car Porters. But their efforts were thwarted at every turn, and they did not begin to meet with success until well into the next century.

These stories of exploitation were not unusual. Workers everywhere had similar stories to tell: the Italian tenement family of seven (including children as young as three and four), who made artificial flowers at home for a meager payment of ten cents for every 144 flowers; cloak makers "slaving for starvation wages," who were forced to sign a pledge not to complain about their work; female workers at Amoskeag textile mill in Manchester, New Hampshire, who had no way to defend themselves against male bosses, who, as one employee complained, "chased the girls and slapped their behinds and sent away the ones they didn't like."

Was it any wonder that workers were weary and bitter? The nation was making great industrial progress, but that progress often seemed to be inseparable from the poverty and degradation of millions who were denied decent wages for their labor—even though their labor had enabled the few on top to gain so much. How could workers receive fair treatment when the wealthy held all the power? Big-business owners and management could do whatever they wanted. They could pay low wages, treat their employees with no regard, and fire an individual or even an entire factory full of people at any time. The continual influx of immigrants assured that there were always more men, women, and children begging for jobs. Before the end of the century, few laws existed to protect the workers, and besides, employers had allies in government and in the courts.

Early attempts at organizing labor unions to engage in collective bargaining for "bread and butter issues"—decent wages, hours, and working conditions—were, for the most part, met by employers with scorn and outrage. One industrialist, president of a press company, claimed that rather than bend to any employees' demands or even enter into discussion with them he "would rather go out of business." It was unthinkable that workers could "cheat" their employers by

Fruit pickers in a southern California orange grove
Seaver Center for Western History Research, Natural History Museum of Los Angeles County

asking to get twelve hours' pay for fewer hours of work. Moreover, many people believed that hard physical labor helped the soul along the path to righteousness and salvation; a short workday was irreligious to their way of thinking. When workers did try to rise up and organize they were usually swiftly defeated. Riots sometimes resulted; most of the time they were instigated by management or police, but the increasing display of violence damaged the reputation of unions in the eyes of the public.

It was only during the last decade of the century that serious attention was paid to the plight of the exploited worker, including women laborers. One woman wrote a report on working conditions in Massachusetts and described women workers packed like "sardines in a box," confined to unventilated attics and damp and cold basements, and forced to use unsanitary toilet facilities "amidst sickening smells." Women were textile mill workers and laundresses who toiled without rest. They were fur workers and feather and cotton sorters handling materials that gave off dust, which caused bronchial illnesses. They worked in soap factories and had hands eaten by caustic chemicals and fingers that were raw and bleeding. When a wound was dressed, the cost of the dressing was charged to the injured.

In 1890, nearly 4 million women worked outside the home. The industrial revolution had created new services for society, which in turn gave women new job opportunities—in shops, offices, telephone companies, restaurants, hotels, beauty shops, and hospitals. Nursing was not yet a respected profession, though, as schoolteaching was. But despite a teacher's respectable work, a woman was paid far less than a man. In New York City in 1898, female schoolteachers received a yearly wage of $600. Men received close to $900. (The reported national average wage of a man in manufacturing was $587, while a woman's was $314.)

Women schoolteachers had other battles to fight too. In Massachusetts, one woman, who had taught for fifteen years, visited friends in another town for Thanksgiving. When she returned she was fired because she had stepped into a carriage with a man who was not her father or brother and she had left town without getting permission from the school board. Other local rules in that district prohibited a woman teacher from marrying, staying out after 8:00 P.M., loitering downtown in an ice cream store, smoking, dressing in bright colors, dyeing her hair, and wearing a dress higher than two inches above the ankle.

Women who worked on farms and ranches and raised families as well often felt isolated and lonely. Many had long worked at various

Workers in the spinning room of the Cornell Mill at Fall River, Massachusetts
U.S. National Archives

other jobs, too, but in the 1890s more began working outside their homes. They ran boardinghouses and hotels, rode the range, or trained horses. Luzena Wilson started a hotel in Nevada City in a tent, setting out a big tureen of soup for her first meals. Mary Fields, born a slave in Tennessee, took a job as a freight hauler out West, then ran a restaurant, drove a stagecoach, carried the U.S. mail, and opened a laundry business. The resourceful Fields was reported to be a mighty fast draw, too.

Generally, black women found few new opportunities open to them and, if they were hired, they were paid less than other women. Mostly they were permitted to work as maids, hairdressers, laundresses, or midwives helping to deliver infants. Shunned from skilled occupations, many in the South—young and old—were concentrated in agriculture, particularly in the tedious job of tobacco stripping.

Children had been caught up in the labor system since the start of industrial days to help the struggling family. Sometimes, children as young as seven or eight were put to work in textile mills, coal mines, farms, canning plants, and glassblowing factories. Their hours were as long as those of adults, and often their toil was as backbreaking. In one southern mill, girls were kept awake at night by splashes of cold water on the face. In an eastern canning factory, boys and girls were required to work sixteen hours a day and cap forty bottles a minute to keep pace with the speed of the assembly line machinery. A glassblowing factory hired orphan boys as young as possible so they could be "trained early and develop the finest skills."

Between 1880 and 1900, some 2 to 3 million children under sixteen worked in America. A few states had passed laws attempting to regulate the minimum age—by 1899, nine states prohibited children under fourteen from working—and some states set arbitrary standards against working under hazardous conditions. Recognizing "the evil of night work," some reformers called for a maximum number of hours in which children were allowed to work. But those laws were wholly inadequate and nearly impossible to enforce. Children at labor didn't attend school. They rarely saw sunshine or played or laughed with friends. Early in their lives they were crushed in body and soul. A man who pioneered the manufacturing and bottling of soft drinks and who used children in running his factory, remarked, "The most beautiful sight we see is the child at labor; as early as he may get at [it] the more beautiful, the more useful does his life become."

In 1893, the country was in the midst of hard economic times. George Pullman and his Palace Car Company were not suffering as some businesses were, but he decided to reduce his expenses anyway. He laid off a portion of his work force and cut the wages of those who remained. But he also continued to charge them the same prices for their lodging and services in his company town. When his employees questioned this unfair pratice, Pullman replied that there was no connection between his roles as employer and landlord.

Throughout 1893 to 1894, Pullman workers gradually organized themselves, forming branches of the American Railway Union (ARU), a recently established national labor union. The ARU was led by Eugene V. Debs, a passionate and fierce fighter for workers' rights, who hoped to build a union of all railroad workers. The son of French Alsatian parents, Debs grew up in Terre Haute, Indiana, where he first went to work at fourteen scraping grease from freight trains. After a succession of jobs, he finally found his calling as a labor leader because, as he explained, he had a "heart for others." Debs's concern for the common worker eventually prompted him to lead the Socialist party, an economic and political movement mostly fostering the idea of public or common ownership of land, utilities, factories, and other means of production. Debs and other party members believed a socialist system would protect workers such as the Pullman employees. Socialists opposed the free enterprise system because they believed it led to greed and exploitation. Socialism became a popular movement at the end of the century.

Encouraged by the ARU's support, Pullman workers chose a committee to discuss their grievances with George Pullman, but he refused to see them, although he promised not to lay off any members of the committee. The next day, however, he fired three members. The laborers were furious, and a protest strike was called. The union proposed arbitration, hoping that a talk between labor and management would peacefully solve the problem, but the company would not negotiate. The workers felt they had no choice but to strike. They refused to handle Pullman cars.

What resulted was widespread disruption of the railroads and chaos, accelerated by the arrival of state militia and then federal armed troops sent by President Grover Cleveland. Finally, full-scale violence

U.S. Infantry troops were called in during the Pullman strike for fair wages and working conditions. The drawing, by Frederic Remington, appeared in Harper's Weekly, 1894.
Illinois State Historical Library, Springfield, Illinois

erupted—looting, fires, and shootings. Debs was arrested on a charge of criminal conspiracy and was sentenced to six months in jail. The union suffered a crushing defeat (just as striking steel workers did at Andrew Carnegie's Homestead mill near Pittsburgh two years earlier). But the spirit of the struggling wage earner was not destroyed. The country was beginning to understand the issues and the need for strong unity and organizational skills and tactics. Among workers, a new confidence and energy emerged. At the turn of the century, working Americans faced the dawn of a new era. Still, it would be many years before union efforts met with real success, however.

Despite continued bitter confrontations, the United Mine Workers (UMW)—which represented coal workers—began to make

Chinese miners in Idaho Springs, Idaho
Denver Public Library, Western History Division

small strides forward. One labor leader, Mary Harris Jones—who came to be called Mother Jones—worked tirelessly on the miners' behalf until her death. She was jailed many times, even as an elderly woman, which only helped win more public sympathy for the cause.

The International Ladies' Garment Workers' Union (ILGWU) formed in 1900 and grew rapidly in membership and determination. In another protest—a most unusual one—Harry Gladstone, a mere fifteen-year-old machine tender and basting puller in a New York jacket sweatshop, found courage to organize seventy-five children to demand a wage increase and a nine-hour workday. When he was interviewed by a newspaper reporter in 1898, Harry, who spoke English and Yiddish, said he wasn't much of a speaker, but

Jewish immigrants sewing knee pants in a tenement sweatshop on Ludlow Street, New York City
Photo by Jacob Riis, Museum of the City of New York

he did have something to tell the children: "If you don't look out for yourselves, who will? You have not had time to grow up, to get strength for work, when you must spend your dearest days in the sweatshop. Think of the way your mothers kiss you, how they love you, and how they shed tears over you, because they see you treated like slaves. . . . The only way to get the bosses to pay us good wages is to stick together, so let us be true to our union."

The most successful and respected union was the American Federation of Labor (AFL) under the leadership of Samuel Gompers, a child of impoverished Dutch Jewish parents, who lived first in England and then in New York City. He entered the world of work as a young shoemaker's apprentice and as a cigar maker alongside his father. Although his formal schooling was cut short, he thrived on political lectures and debates, which he attended as often as he could.

The AFL took a straightforward approach to improving workers' conditions, the most important goal being to preserve and protect the right of collective bargaining by representatives who had been fairly chosen. Eventually, the union also helped achieve the long-sought-after eight-hour day, factory inspections, and workers' compensation for injury. By the turn of the century, half a million AFL members were united, and five years later the union boasted a membership three times that. At first, however, women and unskilled workers were less welcomed into the ranks. Along with black workers, they had a long, trying struggle ahead before they were accepted in the union force.

In 1909, about two hundred workers at the Triangle Shirtwaist Company, where Pauline Newman had worked eighty hours a week, organized and went out on strike. Most of the picketers were young eastern European Jewish and Italian Catholic immigrant women and teenage girls, many the sole support of their families. They could ill afford to lose their wages, no matter how small. Local (chapter) 25 of the ILGWU was badly in need of funds and, therefore, unable to substantially help the women, but the local urged and supported the strike. They were soon joined by sympathetic members of the Women's Trade Union League, a federation of women that had organized six years earlier. The Triangle Company management wanted to "protect its rights" against the women, and hired outside agitators to harass and beat up the picketers. Many of the women were arrested and jailed. Little was accomplished for the strikers that year, but thousands of women elsewhere—shirtwaist makers and garment workers—were inspired to unite in their efforts.

One spring day two years later, on a Saturday near closing time at the Triangle Shirtwaist Company, which occupied the top three floors of a ten-story building, a fire started on the eighth floor. Within

Women laborers marching in a demonstration sponsored by the Women's Trade Union League, New York City, about 1910
Archives of Labor and Urban Affairs, Wayne State University

minutes it had spread so rapidly that attempts to put it out and warn the workers on the ninth and tenth floors were hopeless. There was only panic and hysteria as workers tried to escape. And many did not. By the time the fire department had everything under control, 146 people were dead. They had either burned in the fiery trap or, hair and clothes aflame, had jumped from the windows to their ghastly deaths.

The doors on the eighth floor had been locked, except for one that the women had to exit through for purse inspection to make sure they were not stealing factory garments. The building stairwells and fire escape, which crumbled, were found to have been improperly designed. At the time, New York City required no fire drills. The two Triangle Shirtwaist Company owners were indicted on manslaughter charges, but at their trial they were acquitted. The verdict brought cries of outrage. The tragedy had struck deep, and everywhere people rose up and banded together for the workers' cause. One of those was Pauline Newman, who would dedicate fifty-six years as a worker for the ILGWU.

Children were not given any consideration at the start of the labor movement. Certainly they couldn't stand up for their rights. Although early legislation for them consisted of random statutory provisions to regulate hours and age limits and provide for compulsory education, the laws were weak and ineffective. Massachusetts was one of the first states to recognize some needs of the child worker, including that of education. The state's initial schooling law, however, required only three months a year of schooling for a child under fifteen. Besides, all legislation involved only isolated restrictions and not the complete abolishment of child labor.

Even though Americans increasingly favored some protective laws, opposition to ending child labor was strong, especially during times when the country suffered economic troubles. Bosses wanted to run their businesses freely without government interference. Manufacturers recited any number of reasons why children should be employed. "Children shouldn't be barred from work," said one, "because it builds character, makes them good sober citizens, and provides training to run the nation's industries." One southern textile mill owner insisted that "the dangers of child idleness are as great or greater than the damage of child labor." Another added, "If children of mills are allowed to loaf around the streets, their morals will be corrupted . . . work is for the good of the children and for the good of the people." When the AFL began to push for legislation, it sent agents to various states to help get the legislation passed. In the South, the union was accused of "stirring up trouble in cahoots with the New

England mills so those mills would gain an edge over southern cotton production."

Beginning in 1912, Congress finally held a series of hearings on the subject of child labor and then called for a thorough report, which eventually totaled several volumes. Even then, resistance to federal child labor laws was as strong as ever. Many people still argued that child labor was a state, not a national, issue.

Reformers continued to fight against the shame of child exploitation by big business, however. The Reverend Edgar G. Murphy, a Protestant Episcopal minister in Montgomery, Alabama, led the way in forming the National Child Labor Committee. It was one of the most important organizations in furnishing leadership, influencing people to support the cause, and undertaking research necessary to pass laws that would end child labor and promote compulsory education.

Despite years of setbacks, the American worker at the end of the century was earning new recognition. But the power of unions to improve industrial working conditions would not be fully realized until some three decades later.

6

A Nation of Nations

$\mathbf{T}$hirteen-year-old Mashke Antin lived with her family in the desperately poor Russian village of Polotzk. The Antins were Jewish, and Jews suffered endless persecution throughout Russia. Only a few children were permitted to attend school, and all boys were forced into lengthy military service for the czar and were prohibited from practicing their religion. When a cholera epidemic swept through the region, medicine was dispensed to the gentiles but not to the Jews. In Russia, the Jews lived in constant fear of being attacked and murdered by the czar's soldiers. There was no hope for them in their own country. They dreamed only of a new life in the Promised Land— America.

Mashke's father went there first, and after three years he borrowed money and sent for the family. For Mashke, "the boundaries burst. The arch of heaven soared. A million suns shone out for every star. The winds rushed in from outer space, roaring in my ears, America! America!" In the new land, Mashke was called Mary. Mary

Antin remembered many joys and some disappointments, too, at her "second birth" in Boston, Massachusetts.

Our initiation into American ways began with the first step on the new soil. My father found occasion to instruct or correct us even on the way from the pier to Wall Street, which journey we made crowded together in a rickety cab. He told us not to lean out of the windows, not to point, and explained the word "greenhorn." We did not want to be "greenhorns," and gave the strictest attention to my father's instructions.

The first meal was an object lesson of much variety. My father produced several kinds of food, ready to eat, without any cooking, from little tin cans that had printing all over them. He attempted to introduce us to a queer, slippery kind of fruit, which he called banana, but had to give up for the time being. After the meal, he had better luck with a curious piece of furniture on runners, which he called rocking chair. There were five of us newcomers, and we found five different ways of getting into the American machine of perpetual motion, and as many ways of getting out of it. One born and bred to the use of a rocking chair cannot imagine how ludicrous people can make themselves when attempting to use it for the first time.

In the evening of the first day my father conducted us to the public baths. As we moved along in a little procession, I was delighted with the illumination of the streets. So many lamps, and they burned until morning, my father said, and so people did not need to carry lanterns. In America then, everything was free, as we had heard in Russia. Light was free; the streets were as bright as a synagogue on a holy day. Music was free; we had been serenaded, to our gaping delight, by a brass band of many pieces, soon after our installation on Union Place.

Education was free. That subject my father had written about repeatedly, as comprising his chief hope for us children, the essence of American opportunity, the treasure that no thief could touch, not even misfortune or poverty. It was the one thing that he was able to promise us when he sent for us; surer, safer than bread or shelter. On our second day I was thrilled with the realization of what this freedom of education meant. A little girl from across the alley came and offered to conduct us to school. My father was out, but we five between us had a few words of English by this time. We knew the word "school." We understood. This child, who had never seen us till yesterday, who could not pronounce our names, who was not much better dressed than we, was able to offer us the freedom of the schools of Boston! No application made, no question asked, no examinations, no fees. The doors stood open for every one of us. The smallest child could show us the way.

We had to wait until the opening of the schools in September. What a loss of precious time—from May till September! Not that the time was really lost. Even the interval on Union Place was crowded with lessons and experiences. We had to visit the stores and be dressed from head to foot in American clothing; we had to learn the mysteries of the iron stove, the washboard, and the speaking tube; we had to learn to trade with the fruit peddler through the window, and not to be afraid of the policeman; and, above all, we had to learn English.*

A historian once explained that he started out to write a history of immigrants in America but soon "discovered that the immigrants *were* American history." Between 1815 and 1900, more than 17 million immigrants came to the Promised Land, fleeing persecution, oppression, or starvation caused by a growing European population and a subsequent loss of land. Immigrants gave up their old ways of life for the new and strange, so that they could seek economic freedom and opportunities. Once in America, they worked to settle the nation's farms and frontier, built its transportation and cities, and developed its industries. The immigrant was the main source of the country's labor. Mass immigration—an early wave mostly of English, Irish, German, Dutch, and Scandinavians, followed by a wave of newcomers from Italy, Greece, Austria-Hungary, Russia, Rumania, and Turkey—resulted in the greatest migration in human history. It also brought together a blend of cultures, language, and backgrounds unlike any known to humankind before or since.

*The Promised Land, autobiography of Mary Antin, Boston: Houghton Mifflin, 1911.

Hans J. Dahl family members, immigrants from Norway, settled in their home in Lac Qui Parle, Minnesota. Minnesota Historical Society

The story of the American immigrant is the story of many changes. It is a story of ethnic peoples adapting to alien and confusing ways, while still holding dearly onto Old World values. But it is also a woven pattern of stories about remarkable individuals.

The first English words that Italian-born and educated Constantine Panunzio learned upon arriving in America were "peek and shuvle," and he practiced them proudly. But when he found out that pick and shovel work was about the only kind of work available to Italians, his heart sank. Constantine and several friends had been brought over from Italy by a *padrone*, a labor contractor who took advantage of new immigrants and kept them long in debt for his services. The workers suffered at their menial labor, and many returned to Italy at the first chance. In fact, between the 1880s and the first decade of the 1900s, many thousands of immigrants returned to their home-lands. Certainly, not all immigrants were able to rise successfully, but

Constantine Panunzio was one who did. He first signed on in a lumbering camp, but he was fired because he was no good at wielding an axe. Then he worked in a factory, but that, too, failed because he got caught up in fights among various immigrant groups. He found work again in a lumber camp, this time as an assistant cook (a "cookie"), but he was never paid his promised salary of fifteen dollars a month. At last, he found his "genuine American home" on a farm in Maine. By that time, Constantine was twenty. He enrolled in a school, where he had to sit with children aged six to fourteen, who teased and tormented him—a thoroughly humiliating experience. The sympathetic teacher understood and arranged for him to have private lessons at home. In time, the family for whom he worked helped him get a scholarship to a private high school, and he went on to graduate from college.

In the mountainous Greek village where Nicholas Gerros lived, every day was a struggle for the most basic needs. To make matters worse, taxes were so high that no one could afford to pay them. Moreover, Greece was part of the Ottoman Empire—under Turkish rule—and by law all Greek boys were forced to go into Turkish military service, which the Greeks resented. Maybe Nicholas could have a better chance in America, his parents thought. So, when Nicholas was fourteen, they arranged for his passage. Upon his arrival, he was given a Bible and a church pamphlet printed in English, which he couldn't read, as well as his first taste of ice cream. He was then taken to live in an apartment in Cincinnati, Ohio, with several other Greek boys, all of whom were put to work in a shoemaker's shop. One day, Nicholas passed some other boys his age on the street, and they began to taunt him because he couldn't speak English. He tried to move along, but they grabbed him and beat him bloody. That was when Nicholas made up his mind to enroll in school and learn English. He also decided to go to a place he had heard about where he could learn to defend himself—the YMCA. After years of struggle, including a bout with tuberculosis, he moved to New Hampshire. There, he eventually succeeded in the men's clothing business and became an active community member, as well as an executive at the local YMCA.

Most immigrants experienced profound shock when they arrived. They were herded, prodded, and examined. They felt lost because they were unable to communicate in English, lacked a continuity of daily life, and were lonely and alienated from American society at nearly every turn. They were strangers to the political process and were unfamiliar with American political issues. They were vulnerable and trusting, usually unaware of their legal rights, which made them easy prey for those who took advantage of them. Their ethnic and mostly peasant backgrounds determined the jobs they could secure at the start—usually unskilled, menial work—and the neighborhoods in which they would live. They crowded in with people of similar ethnic backgrounds in city slums, although hundreds of thousands settled in the Plains states and Texas. And in their new homes and at their new jobs, many learned that their dreams had to be reshaped, perhaps to be realized only by their children or grandchildren.

The new immigrant was sustained by family, religion, and school. Family members offered much support to one another. Sometimes they even worked together, on a farm, or at home making cigars or artificial flowers, or as "sweaters"—sewing piecework that was subcontracted out from a factory. Though there was little enough sleeping space in the crowded tenements—at night, many kitchens were transformed into bedrooms—the immigrant always managed to find a corner for a newly arrived sister, cousin, or uncle.

Religion also helped to preserve ethnic and cultural ties. The church and synagogue became the center of immigrant communities, providing not only spiritual comfort but also a gathering place for social events. School became a bridge between the Old and New worlds. After long, exhausting hours at work, many adults found renewed energy to attend a night class so they could learn English. Children were eager to study, and they learned quickly. One girl said that school filled her with excitement every day, and so did the simple

Lugo family members in Bell, California, about 1890, after an earlier generation migrated from Mexico. Before the turn of the century, a few thousand Latin Americans crossed the border and settled in the southwestern states. Between 1900 and 1930, about three-quarters of a million immigrants came to live and work in the United States.
Seaver Center for Western History Research, Natural History Museum of Los Angeles County

act of carrying books—"the bigger the stack, the more wonderful." Another girl adored her teacher with the "heavenly name of Elizabeth A. Bliss," who lived in a neighborhood where she kept a garden and who on spring days brought an armful of fragrant peonies to school. Mary Antin, who became a gifted student and writer, learned to read in a small class while a teacher "aided us so skillfully and earnestly in our endeavors to 'see-a-cat,' 'hear-dog-bark,' and 'look-at-the-hen,' that we turned over page after page of the ravishing history, eager to find out how the common world looked, smelled, and tasted in the strange speech."

Immigrant children attending New York City's Mott Street Industrial School learn to pledge their allegiance to the United States. The classroom flag salute became part of the immigrant experience beginning in 1892. Photo by Jacob Riis, Museum of the City of New York

Immigrant children became Americanized more quickly than their mothers and fathers, and this widened the distance between parent and child and often unraveled the fabric of the once-close family. In Polotzk, Mary Antin's parents had constantly watched their children and had instilled in them a code of conduct and ethics, but in America, the children were "let loose on the street," Mary said, "and chaos took the place of system. My parents knew only that they desired us to be like American children; and seeing how their neighbors gave their children boundless liberty, they turned us also loose, never doubting but that the American way was the best. . . . They had no standards to go by, seeing that America was not Polotzk. In their bewilderment and uncertainty they [trusted] us to children to learn from such models as the tenements afforded. More than this, they must step down from their throne of parental authority. This sad process of disintegration of home life may be observed in almost any immigrant family of our class and with our traditions and aspirations. It is part of the process of Americanization."

It was difficult enough for the newcomers to learn American customs and manners, adjust to the country's political and legal systems, and discover the new land itself. Many also had to deal with ethnic and religious prejudice and bigotry, which became more pervasive as the flow of immigration increased. Because of prejudice and discrimination, Italians had limited choices of work; ads for workers sometimes stated that "Irish need not apply," and signs were hung outside establishments reading: "No colored, Jews, or dogs allowed." As in Russia, Jews experienced anti-Semitism in their adopted country too. Intolerance also existed among Jews themselves: Some of the German Jews who arrived earlier behaved as if they were superior to the Jews arriving later from eastern Europe. During the 1890s, Catholics were also targets of hostility. At one point, pamphlets were widely circulated expressing fear that Catholics "would swell so greatly in number that they would take over the land."

But of all the late-nineteenth-century newcomers, the Chinese suffered the worst treatment. Many Americans believed that the customs of the Chinese immigrants were so different that they were incapable of assimilating into Western society. Most Chinese residents were men who had escaped famine and civil war at home, and who hoped to make money and return to China. They were mocked, beaten, and murdered by gangs of hoodlums. An elderly man who ran a laundry in California explained that every Saturday night he lived in fear of white miners who got drunk and forced their way into the shop, destroying customers' sheets and shirts, for which he was responsible. One night, a drunken miner slammed his own face into an iron. He became so enraged that he stormed out of the shop, threatening to return. The launderer knew his life was in danger and fled. Later that night, he learned that the miner had returned with a mob, which ransacked and set the laundry on fire.

Anti-Chinese feelings ran so high that in 1882 the United States established the Chinese Exclusion Act, which blocked Chinese immigration for ten years and forbade their becoming naturalized residents. It was renewed for another ten years. Intolerance toward the Chinese extended to the Japanese, who began to immigrate after 1900.

By the end of the century, immigration became a national political issue, dividing people throughout the country. America was a great nation of nations, but nevertheless, the outcries of American-born people known as nativists, who were sharply critical of continued mass immigration, rang out loud. They feared not only the loss of their jobs, but the possibility that "poor and illiterate immigrants would debase American life and bring down the image of the American worker." They criticized foreigners for segregating themselves in neighborhoods among their own, which "prevented them from becoming Americanized." Some Americans were simply uncomfortable working side by side with people who were "different."

John Mitchell, president of the United Mine Workers, spoke for the nativists, saying, "No matter how decent and self-respecting and hardworking the aliens who are flooding this country may be, they are invading the land of Americans, and whether they know it or not, are helping to take bread out of their mouths. America for Americans should be the motto of every citizen. . . . There is not enough work for the many millions of unskilled laborers, and there is no need for the added millions who are pressing into our cities and towns to compete with the skilled American in his various trades and occupations." This competition for work and food was the very problem that had scourged European and Asian countries, forcing millions of their citizens to set out for America in the first place.

Political cartoon depicting immigrants turned nativists "closing to the newcomers the bridge that carried them and their fathers over" to America. The lithograph by Joseph Keppler, 1892, is titled "Looking Backward."
Library of Congress

Foreign workers were attacked on both economic and political fronts. More and more violence erupted in the workplace, especially when economic times were bad. A group of miners and townspeople, including foreigners and American-born, was killed during a strike in southern Colorado's coal fields, a saloon keeper was stabbed to death and six foreigners were implicated in the murder; and a group of farmers rampaged against Jewish merchants in a Louisiana town.

In 1900, one writer described America as a nation in which everyone is an immigrant or a descendant of an immigrant, and where the peoples of all races and religions have come together to form a new and common culture. He called America a melting pot. Some found this to be a meaningful expression and concept, while others were left uneasy. But everyone reflected on the question: What is an American? It was a difficult question to answer.

One man, Carl Schurz, a German immigrant who rose to prominence as senator from Missouri and secretary of the interior of the U.S. government, said in a speech: "To me the word Americanism, true Americanism, comprehends the noblest ideas which ever swelled a human heart with noble pride. Under this banner [American democracy] all the languages of civilized mankind are spoke, every creed is protected, every right is sacred. . . . This is true Americanism, clasping mankind to its great heart. Under its banner we march; let the world follow."

7

Rise of the City

On the evening of October 8, 1871, on the southwest side of Chicago a peg-legged man named Sullivan was sitting on the boardwalk at De Koven Street. It was a warm night and since there had been little rain that year, it was unusually dry. Suddenly Sullivan saw a lick of flame coming from the O'Leary cow shed across the street. "Fire!" he shouted, alerting the neighborhood. By the time an engine company with a hose cart arrived, the cow shed was ablaze and the fire was starting to spread.

In the confusion that followed, there were delays in dispatching further assistance. Besides, the fire department was not in full force that night, nor was all the equipment available because the men had battled a gigantic fire only days before. Much of the city, which had grown steadily over the previous decades as the heartland of the prairie, was built of wood. Now, increasing winds fanned the flames, which soon began to leap north and east. The fire quickly raged out of control, and panic set in. People fled farther north toward Lincoln Park and Lake Michigan.

The fire burned for more than twenty-four hours. Nearly three hundred people perished. The entire downtown district—banks, public buildings, hotels, businesses, railroad depots, churches—and most of the residential North Side were wiped out. A hundred thousand people were left homeless.

Legend has it that the O'Learys' cow started the great Chicago fire when she kicked over a kerosene lamp. But that is not proven fact. Whatever the cause, the city that had been the "world's busiest corner" lay in rubble and ruin. Some thought it doomed, its glory gone forever, while others claimed that all was not lost. "We shall build again!" the hopeful cried. One local man predicted, "The business houses will be rebuilt, and by the year 1900 the new Chicago will boast a population of a million souls. . . . I know that the location of Chicago makes her the center of this wealthy region. . . . . What Chicago has been in the past, she must become in the future and hundred fold more."

Out of the ashes the city rose again. Assistance arrived from all directions in the way of food, clothing, shelter, money, bank loans, and investments. President Ulysses S. Grant sent a personal check for a thousand dollars. Little by little, Chicago began to rebuild—from the small real estate agent who put up a shack with a sign, "All gone but wife, children, and energy," to the farm machinery magnate, Cyrus McCormick, whose harvest reaper plant had been destroyed, but who at once started rebuilding on a large scale.

Up went a new courthouse and city hall, department stores, factories, and warehouses. Up went the McVicker's Theater and the Palmer House Hotel. By 1890, Chicago's population topped a million. Then, in 1893, the city hosted the World's Columbian Exposition, an extravagant international fair, to mark the four hundredth anniversary of Christopher Columbus's arrival in the New World and to show off Chicago's accomplishments. Chicago had become a vital new city, bursting with pride.

Industrial America had developed rapidly as a nation, but the

American city had grown even faster. Masses of immigrants poured forth, and a vast population shifted from the country to the city. Between 1860 and 1900, the rural population had doubled, but the number of city dwellers had quadrupled! The city became the supreme achievement of modern industry, the center of civilization during the Gilded Age. It spread outward and reached upward, embracing mechanized factories and the corporate business world,

ghettos for the poor and suburbs for the middle class, exclusive neighborhoods for the wealthy and ethnic neighborhoods for the immigrants.
In addition to its continual pursuit of industrial progress, the city also
created cultural opportunities in literature, music, art, architecture,
dance, and theater. And it built parks for pleasure and recreation.

The new symbol of achievement was the skyscraper. Before the
development of the skyscraper, the discerning viewed city architecture
as unattractive and unimaginative. Factories, stores, and housing had
the same drab look. The first real skyscraper, the ten-story Home
Insurance Building in Chicago, was designed by William le Baron

The Wainwright Building in St. Louis, Missouri, early skyscraper designed by famed architect Louis Sullivan
Library of Congress

Jenney, who used the revolutionary principle of the steel skeleton. An architect named Louis Sullivan, described as having the "analytical mind of a scientist and the soul of a dreamer and artist," enhanced early basic steel-frame construction and set the style of lofty, airy sky-scrapers for decades to come.

The city offered hope and opportunity, but it also brought despair. Despite its new stature and pride, Chicago shared with cities like New York, Boston, Philadelphia, Pittsburgh, St. Louis, and Minneapolis overwhelming social problems: poverty, disease, crime, and conflict between powerful business leaders and exploited workers.

Big-city problems were often called evils, and among the worst were the slums, the neighborhoods of the desperately overcrowded poor. Slum dwellers lived in bleak, airless tenement buildings. These tenements were foul and infested, traps for both fires and deadly contagious diseases like tuberculosis, diphtheria, and scarlet fever. The struggling poor lived with sewage pollution and impure water; their meager diets could not begin to provide them with necessary nutrition. In the tenements, disease and death were rampant.

In New York City, where more than half the population lived in slums—known by such names as Bottle Alley, Hell's Kitchen, and Bandit's Roost—there were attempts made to improve the tenements. "Dumb-bell" style buildings were designed and built with air shafts leading from the ground to the roof in the structure's center to allow for air and light. But the air shafts made matters worse. They carried up odors from all the garbage and filth strewn about, and if a fire broke out, the shaft caused flames to rush upward and consume the building in a matter of minutes.

In one section of Mulberry Street, forty families were packed into five dilapidated houses that had been built to hold one family each. In a Cherry Street tenement one winter day, a man who had contracted a respiratory disease and could no longer work as a seaman, was found shivering in a rented room along with his wife and three children. The parents slept on the floor, the two older children in boxes, and the baby swung in a shawl attached to the ceiling rafters by cords. In another district, a ragged boy selling newspapers crawled into a basement ventilation chute one night to get warm and was burned to death when a fire broke out. In yet another district, a child named Mary Ellen had been so brutally beaten by her parents that she couldn't walk and was carried into the police station wrapped in a horse blanket. Later in court, a judge wanted to send her to a hospital, but he had no legal authority because parents had total legal rights over their children. Every day, slum dwellers asked themselves how they could go on living.

"The poorest immigrant comes here with the purpose and ambition to better himself and, given half a chance, might be reasonably expected to make the most of it. To the false plea that he prefers the squalid homes in which his kind are housed there could be no better answer. The truth is, his half chance has too long been wanting, and for the bad result he has been unjustly blamed."

Such sympathy and understanding was expressed by a man who devoted much of his life toward the cause of cleaning up city slums and giving "half a chance" to people who could not escape their misery by themselves. His name was Jacob Riis. He had immigrated from Denmark and for years had wrestled valiantly at menial labor and at learning English until he finally found satisfaction and success as a newspaper reporter in New York City. His first assignments were police beat stories. Scouting the city's many neighborhoods at all hours of the day and night, he came face to face with the wretched poverty, crime, and hopelessness endured by the struggling immigrants.

Riis felt both grief and outrage, and often he became so emotionally overwrought that he wondered if he shouldn't find other work. But he knew that he must use his talents as a writer—and later as a photographer—to make the public aware of those who needed help and who could no longer be ignored. So he wrote story after story in newspapers and magazines, dramatically describing what he saw and heard, purposely tugging at his readers' hearts. He detailed dingy buildings with rotting wood floors and air "fouler than the mud of the gutters; an alley full of filthy beggars, ragpickers, and dirty, hungry children playing with a dripping water hydrant, their only amusement."

Riis also called the public to replace tenements with improved living conditions; to fight corruption at the hands of landlords, labor and business management, and city political-machine bosses; to investigate violations of laws enacted to protect workers in factories and sweatshops; to improve health and sanitation by purifying polluted city water supplies; to provide parks and playgrounds for deprived

Slum scene photo by Jacob Riis, taken at the Baxter Street tenement Museum of the City of New York

children, whom he held dearest to his heart. Many of these reforms that Riis and other crusading individuals and organizations called for, such as the Society for the Prevention of Cruelty to Children, were eventually achieved, but they were painfully slow in coming.

Another city evil was crime: street crime such as theft, robbery, and violence committed against citizens; organized crime by gangs such as the Molasses Gang and the Dutch Mob, who targed mostly businesses and other organizations with terror, blackmail, and murder; and corrupt practices by city government officials. City bosses often preyed upon new immigrants and the struggling poor, feigning sincere friendship with the innocent and offering gifts like free holiday turkeys in exchange for their votes. In a book called *The Shame of the Cities*, writer Lincoln Steffens, another reform journalist, exposed graft, swindles, gambling, padded payrolls, and other vices such as special privileges for the wealthy. Steffens wrote, "Politics is business. That's the matter with it." He decried city leaders who cared about their own success above social ideals.

San Francisco was the fastest growing city in the West, thanks to the mid-century gold rush. But while its population swelled and its commerce boomed—resulting in the widespread construction of ornately decorated public buildings and private mansions and a vast garden plaza in the center of town—the city faced its own peculiar problems. Because of its unruly saloon and dance-hall life, gambling, shootings, and gun duels at dawn, San Francisco became known as "the wickedest city on earth." This lawlessness prompted good citizens to take the law into their own hands. From time to time, they succeeded in running an outlaw out of town, but the vigilante groups alone could not rid the city of its crime.

The era inspired many reformers who aimed to arouse the social conscience of their fellow citizens for the betterment of society. They worked for municipal improvements and sought educational reforms, big-business reforms, and political reforms, such as replacing political-machinery nominations and appointments of candidates with direct public primaries, direct election of senators, and direct election of delegates to national nominating conventions. They advocated public health care and prison reform. They fought for children's rights and women's rights, including the right to vote. Under the leadership of Frances Willard, the Woman's Christian Temperance Union (WCTU) tried to do away with the sale and consumption of alcohol, which it saw as an evil, in order to save the "real victim of alcoholism —the family." And of course, socialists, like Eugene V. Debs, continued to campaign for public ownership of land and property.

In Chicago, Jane Addams, a privileged, upper-class woman,

Social worker Jane Addams established Hull House in Chicago to help improve lives of the poor and the displaced. Archives of Labor and Urban Affairs, Wayne State University

revolted against the idea that "the sheltered, educated girl has nothing to do with the bitter poverty and social maladjustment which is all about her." Addams had been to London and had found herself shocked at the living conditions of the poor there, as well as in other cities she had visited. She began to realize that the wealthy could use their resources to help the poor. Longing for an "outward symbol of fellowship, some bond of peace, some blessed spot where unity of spirit might claim right of way over all differences," she and a friend set out to establish an institution that would fulfill her longings as well as the needs of others.

On South Halsted Street, near stockyards and a shipyard, and amidst a wide range of immigrant groups, they opened a community center, or settlement house for the poor. They called their settlement—a large, old house—Hull House, and offered youth clubs, child care, reading, musical and theater groups, as well as a place for people of different backgrounds to meet and share ideas and traditions. Hull House prospered because of Addams's skilled organizational abilities and the continued support of privileged women whom Addams attracted as both staff members and contributors of money. The settlement became the model for others that were established in cities everywhere, and Addams was recognized as a pioneer in community social work.

In New York City in 1895, the mayor offered a young political figure the position of head of the street-cleaning department, but the politician declined, explaining that he had no special fitness for that department. He then accepted an appointment on the police commission and served two years as the commission's president. The man was Theodore Roosevelt.

It so happened that Roosevelt had read a book, *How the Other Half Lives*, by Jacob Riis, and found it "an enlightenment and an inspiration." Roosevelt was a great reader, a man who liked to get things done, a man who believed that words ought to be translated into deeds. He wrote a letter to Riis complimenting him on his work and offering the help of the police and health departments to right some of the city's wrongs.

The two men came from vastly different backgrounds. Unlike Riis, a penniless immigrant, Roosevelt grew up amidst wealth and luxury and was educated at Harvard University. He had been a sickly child, but he fought to overcome a severe asthma condition and eventually triumphed. He blossomed into an extraordinarily athletic and rugged individual. Despite their differing pasts, the men shared similar ideals and moral purposes in life, and when they met they became fast friends. Early in their friendship, Roosevelt appeared at Riis's office one day, shouting good-naturedly, "Hello, Jake! What do we do first?" Riis took Roosevelt around the city, showing him the heartbreaking sights so long familiar to the journalist. Roosevelt's energy matched Riis's, and at once the dynamic Roosevelt took it upon himself to bring about many city reforms, including weeding out corruption and increasing efficiency in the police force, and ordering saloons ("a chief source of mischief") closed on Sundays. The police department received several letters from grateful mothers, commenting that for the first time their husbands were willing to take their families on Sunday outings. Efforts to limit wicked and immoral conduct were far more difficult. Later, after Roosevelt left the police department, some of the corrupt practices among city officials crept back. But his accomplishments as law enforcer demonstrated that a strong agency in charge could control a fair amount of crime.

At the turn of the century, the American city began to see new economic problems because businesses were no longer expanding as fast as before. Railroad construction and mining development had slowed. On the whole, wages were not rising fast enough, and consumption of manufactured goods lagged. What was needed, according to theorists, was new investment in productive enterprises.

Meanwhile, the American city itself continued to stretch. The towering skyscraper, the skyline at dawn, the graceful span of a bridge, the sprawling park dotted with blossoming trees—all were becoming part of a larger and grander metropolitan vision.

8

Souls of Black Folk

It was a cold February night in 1898. In the small town of Lake City, South Carolina, members of the Baker family lay sleeping in their house, which also served as the local post office. Mr. Baker had been appointed postmaster, but the people of Lake City didn't like the appointment because Mr. Baker was black. For months, they had been threatening him. A congressman and senator were seeking to have him removed from his job; however, no such action had been taken.

Finally, in the middle of that winter night, a group of armed white men surrounded the Baker house and lit a torch to it. The family awoke, startled, and dashed to escape the first rush of flames. But Mr. Baker didn't have a chance. As soon as he appeared at the doorway, a bullet pierced his skull. Instantly, he fell to his death. Scores of more bullets rang out, killing a baby in Mrs. Baker's arms and injuring three other daughters and a son. The postmaster and infant were cremated in the fire of the burning house.

Law enforcement officials made no effort to arrest or punish the murderers. This was not unusual, though. Throughout the nation, especially in the South, whites ruled with a violent hand; black citizens were murdered outright or by tortuous methods while the law looked the other way.

Slavery had ended during the Civil War, but former slaves were left with a wretched economic heritage. Soon southern states enacted codes that exploited the newly freed at labor. And federal education and land-grant assistance, a huge task to manage, turned out to be short-lived and fraught with problems ranging from confusion and corrupt officials to war-torn, embittered Southerners' opposition to offering help at all. Nevertheless, despite hurdles at every turn, blacks established schools, bought or leased land, built farms, and rose to positions in business and government. Their progress, however, frightened and angered racists, who clung to a long-held idea of white supremacy, who believed that America was a "white man's country." One observer wrote, "The trouble is the Negro is advancing too rapidly for many of the whiteliners of the South, and there is a determination to call a halt. Consequently, all sorts of schemes are devised to impede the progress of the blacks."

During the last decades of the nineteenth century, a widespread segregation movement swept across the nation. The federal government was unwilling to protect the rights of all black citizens, and that encouraged the enactment of local ordinances and state laws denying blacks their rights. Starting in 1915, as life became more difficult in the South, masses of rural blacks migrated to the urban North; however, they were usually relegated to the bottom of the work force, even when their level of education and skills matched that of white immigrants.

Then the South saw the rebirth of an old racist organization, the Ku Klux Klan (KKK), whose members dressed in white hooded sheets and viciously terrorized and murdered black men, women, and children. By the early 1900s, Klan power had spread to northern and western states as well. In trumpeting their racial superiority, Klansmen

◆ The Ku Klux Klan ◆

The Ku Klux Klan, a name derived from a Greek word meaning "circle" or "band," was formed in Pulaski, Tennessee, after the Civil War. It began as a social fraternity of men concerned with maintaining white rule but evolved into a secret society that at first intimidated black citizens and eventually turned to acts of terrorism and violence against them. The KKK, which was concentrated in southern rural areas, also came to be called the Invisible Empire of the South, and it awarded its leaders with such titles as grand wizard, dragon, and cyclops.

Although the federal government made efforts to expose and destroy the Klan and was fairly successful for short periods of time, the KKK emerged even stronger in the South and spread to other states, flourishing as a powerful political force in many regions. Its sharp rise was attributed to growing fears and frustrations stemming from continued black migration to northern states, an influx of immigrants into the labor force, increase in Jewish and Catholic populations, and radical new movements such as communism.

By the second decade of the new century, the Ku Klux Klan boasted a nationwide membership of more than 3 million, with members drawn from all classes of white society in rural and urban areas. It no longer confined itself to secrecy and terrorism but openly conducted activities such as parades and flag-burning rallies. Other organizations imitated the Klan, but the KKK remained the strongest and most notorious.

also attacked white Catholics, Jews, and foreigners. But their first goal was to demoralize blacks and keep them under the economic and political control of whites—in sum, to "re-enslave" them in different ways. The KKK led lynching bands that kidnaped, hanged, burned, and shot black people. They whipped, clubbed, and mutilated them, and had them torn apart by dogs.

Ku Klux Klan, Funeral Degree Team in Sullivan, Indiana, forms a cross at the burial ceremony of a fellow worker.
Indiana State Library

William Sinclair, a black historian, wrote that the refusal of the South to accept the freed black as fully human resulted in an atmosphere where "mobs torture human beings and roast them alive without trial and in defiance of law and order . . . mobs take possession of the streets . . . mobs break into jails and take out prisoners and hang them. . . . " From Arkansas one year came reports of a man burned at the stake, another strung up and riddled with bullets, and a boy forced to confess to a crime that he tearfully protested he didn't commit, yet as soon as he "confessed," he was lynched by a mob. Bent on keeping blacks from becoming educated, lest they become "dangerous," Klan members in a Mississippi county stoned black pupils, publicly whipped their teachers, and later destroyed the schoolhouses. Men in a New Hampshire town chained a tiny schoolhouse to a team of oxen and dragged it into a swamp. In Mayesville, South Carolina, a white man lit a cigarette for himself and ordered a black man nearby to blow out the match. When the man refused, the two got into a fight. A mob gathered at once, dragged the black man away, and hanged him, his cries for mercy ignored. Between 1889 and 1918, some thirty-two hundred black citizens were savagely murdered in the United States.

In 1902, a black Alabama woman published an article, but she wouldn't allow her name to be printed for fear of endangering her life.

> The Southerners say we Negroes are a happy, laughing set of people, with no thought of tomorrow. How mistaken they are! The educated, thinking Negro is just the opposite. There is a feeling of unrest, insecurity, almost panic among the best class of Negroes in the South. In our homes, in our churches, wherever two or three are gathered together, there is a discussion of what is best to do. Must we remain in the South or go elsewhere? Where can we go to feel that security which other people feel? . . .
>
> I know of houses occupied by poor Negroes in which a respectable farmer would not keep his cattle. It is impossible for them to rent elsewhere. All southern real estate agents have "white property" and "colored property. . . ."
>
> Many colored women who wash, iron, scrub, cook or sew all the week [usually in white homes] to help pay the rent for these miserable hovels and help fill the many small mouths, would deny themselves some of the necessaries of life if they could take their little children and teething babies on the cars to the parks on a Sunday afternoon and sit under the trees, enjoy the cool breezes and breathe God's pure air for only two or three hours; but this is denied them. Some of the parks have signs, "No Negroes allowed on these grounds except as servants. . . ."

Laws that forbade blacks to visit parks, ride with whites in streetcars, or walk on downtown sidewalks were called Jim Crow laws. The name came from minstrel shows, in which white actors darkened their faces and performed as blacks, often portraying them as slow or comical. One of those characters was named Jim Crow. First, he became a stereotype for all blacks, then a symbol for segregation.

The Fifteenth Amendment to the U.S. Constitution had granted the right of franchise—the right to vote—to every man. Historian Sinclair called the ballot "the citadel of the colored man's safety, the guarantor of his liberty, the protector of his rights." But instead, great numbers of black men found themselves disfranchised. When they were not forcibly kept from the polls, there were plenty of "schemes . . . devised to impede" them, like property requirements; a poll tax, which many could not afford to pay; or a literacy test, which often included absurd questions or a requirement to recite by memory a long portion of the Constitution.

The turn of the century saw the country's first widespread race riots, with whites attacking blacks in their homes and on the streets. One of the bloodiest took place in Atlanta, Georgia; another in Springfield, Illinois, erupted after a white woman accused a black man of raping her, although she later confessed that she had been violated by a white man whose name she refused to reveal. Riots followed in one state after another, including Oklahoma, New York, North Carolina, and Florida.

Blacks were filled with despair, disillusionment, and outrage. "The real cause of our trouble is race hatred," said Bishop Alexander Walters of the African Methodist Episcopal Zion Church in New York City. "Some years ago it was thought that as the Negroes became intelligent and cultured this race prejudice would disappear; but in some sections of this country it has only intensified this feeling."

Black Americans had hoped to make steady gains, but they found themselves continually struggling in a world intent on halting their progress. The time seemed right, then, for many to speak out; to take political action; to discover their creative abilities as artists, poets, and musicians; and to develop skills and talents too long ignored. The period between 1890 and 1930 became known as the Golden Age of

Black Nationalism. During this time, black churches helped establish more schools and universities; an anti-lynching crusade was started, and blacks formed numerous organizations. Always the leaders spoke out courageously, but in doing so they risked violent opposition from whites.

One educational leader was Mary McLeod Bethune. Once as a child she had accompanied her mother to work in a white family's house. When she picked up a book, the little girl there shouted, "Put down that book! You can't read it!" Mary was deeply hurt, but it wasn't her fault that she couldn't read. There were no public schools for black children in her town. In time, she struggled to receive an education, working exceptionally hard to win scholarship aid to missionary and Bible schools. Bethune went on to become a devoted teacher and eventually founded a school for black girls in Daytona Beach, Florida. Later, she became a presidential adviser on education and black youth and a highly successful leader in the fight for women's rights.

Another activist was Ida B. Wells-Barnett, a woman who began the nation's anti-lynching movement and who spoke out strongly in opposition to Jim Crow. Wells-Barnett started her career as a journalist and soon became editor of a black Memphis, Tennessee, newspaper. Her writings and lectures calling lynching "a national crime," her denunciation of outrageous treatment of blacks, and her appeals for justice aroused public opinion and inspired other black citizens to speak out, too.

Black Nationalism's two most prominent leaders were Booker T. Washington and William Edward Burghardt Du Bois. Washington was born into slavery on a Virginia plantation. After he and his mother were freed, he went to work in a West Virginia salt furnace. During that period, his mother, at considerable expense and sacrifice, bought him an old speller, and he taught himself to read. In time, he heard about the Hampton Institute in Virginia, where blacks could learn a trade, so riding and walking, he set out on a five-hundred-mile journey. At Hampton, he paid his way by working as a janitor after school

Ida B. Wells-Barnett
Illinois State Historical
Library, Old State Capitol,
Springfield, Illinois

hours. He continued studying in Washington, D.C., and then began a distinguished career as an educator. Later, he founded the Tuskegee Institute in Alabama, originally a normal school for teacher training and eventually a school that provided academic and specialized studies. Tuskegee's agriculture research department became world renowned. Washington's autobiography, *Up From Slavery*, was destined to become a classic in American literature.

From his position at Tuskegee, Washington became an articulate spokesman for blacks. He urged them not only to seek an education but to learn vocational and industrial skills for economic survival; to win the confidence and friendship of whites; to wait patiently for eventual acceptance by white society. Washington presented these beliefs in 1895 in a speech that came to be known as the "Atlanta

Booker T. Washington
Tuskegee University,
Tuskegee, Alabama

History class at Tuskegee
Institute, Tuskegee,
Alabama
Library of Congress

Compromise." Washington was widely praised and admired, especially by whites, but he was also highly criticized for his "compromise" views and for so easily accepting white people's dictates. Black critics thought that resolving racial differences with friendliness and patience was unrealistic.

One who disagreed with Washington's approach was W. E. B. Du Bois, a sociologist, historian, and editor; a man who saw black culture as having its own "soul"; a man who thought that blacks risked losing political power and, ultimately, the chance to gain their rights by remaining submissive. He believed that to win those rights blacks ought to be assertive, seeking broad educational opportunities and taking legal recourse. "While it is a great truth to say that the Negro must strive and strive mightily to help himself," he wrote, "it is equally true that unless his striving be not simply seconded, but rather aroused and encouraged by the initiative of the richer and wiser environing group, he cannot hope for success." Whatever their opposing views, Washington and Du Bois both wanted blacks to achieve the same goals; mostly they differed in their ideas of how to reach those goals.

Du Bois grew up with his mother in Great Barrington, Massachusetts. He was a gifted pupil, and after he finished public school, townsfolk from local churches gave him a scholarship to attend Fisk University in Tennessee. He went on to do graduate work at Harvard University, where he was the first black to receive a Ph.D.; then, following years of teaching, he began to shape his life as a black nationalist leader. He studied black ghettos, wrote and spoke extensively about race relations, and demanded good schools, voting rights, and jobs with fair pay for blacks; he voiced outrage against lynchings and Jim Crow. He questioned whites, asking them if their own attitudes and behavior toward blacks might not affect black people in America.

His most widely acclaimed book was *The Souls of Black Folk*, a brilliant collection of essays that discusses human passions, the long frustrating journeys of blacks throughout their lives, the meaning of

W. E. B. Du Bois
Archives of the University
of Massachusetts at
Amherst

their religion, the depth of their sorrow, and the woes of having "to live haunted by the ghost of an untrue dream." He wrote, "One ever feels his two-ness—an American; a Negro; two souls, two thoughts, two unreconciled strivings, two warring ideals in one dark body, whose dogged strength alone keeps it from being torn asunder. The history of the American Negro is the history of this strife—this longing to attain self-conscious manhood, to merge his double self into a better and truer self."

Du Bois and a coalition of black intellectuals formed an organization dedicated to the pursuit of political and economic rights for blacks. It was called the Niagara Movement, and it won the respect and support of a great many people. Although it had little money and offered membership only to black intellectuals, the movement marked a turning point in black organization and power. Eventually, it changed direction under the leadership of a wider range of people, including blacks and whites of both sexes, and became the National

Association for the Advancement of Colored People (NAACP) in 1908. The NAACP emerged as the most effective black organization of the time. Others were the National Urban League, the National Association of Colored Women, and the National Negro Business League.

Although blacks in America were making gains, they were struck a devastating blow just before the end of the century. The story began in Louisiana when a man named Homer Plessy boarded a train in New Orleans one day. After he sat down in a parlor car, he was asked to leave because the car was reserved for whites only. Plessy was one-eighth black. When he refused to move he was arrested for violating a Jim Crow law. In a Louisiana court, Plessy argued that such a law was unconstitutional, but Judge Ferguson, the presiding judge, ruled against him. Plessy appealed his case to higher courts until it reached the United States Supreme Court. There, in 1896, the majority of justices upheld the constitutionality of the Louisiana law. The Court declared that the Constitution referred only to "political" equality, and concluded that separating blacks from whites was acceptable because such action was a "social" matter. Only one justice dissented, arguing that the Constitution was "color-blind."

The decision, eagerly embraced by the white South, made legal a "separate but equal" doctrine regarding public transportation. In short time, this doctrine stretched to include schools, hospitals, hotels, restaurants, cemeteries, public bathrooms, and drinking fountains. But surely there was no equality for blacks. The ruling really meant separate and *un*equal. The ruling established for millions of black Americans a life of segregation that would last for many decades.

"Now behold a century new for the duty and the deed," Du Bois wrote. "The problem of the Twentieth Century is the problem of the color-line."

9

The Family— At Home, at School, at Play

The Wells family lived in a small house in Holly Springs, Mississippi. Mr. and Mrs. Wells had been cotton plantation slaves, but after their emancipation Mrs. Wells worked as a cook and Mr. Wells as a carpenter. They had eight children; the eldest was a daughter named Ida, who later became an outstanding black leader. The Wellses were Christians, and they faithfully attended church and read the Bible together every Sunday afternoon.

But tragedy struck the family. A deadly yellow fever epidemic swept the region. The parents and the baby became ill and died. (Another child had died earlier.) Friends arranged to take in the surviving children, but Ida, sixteen years old at the time, insisted on keeping them together. "After being a lighthearted schoolgirl," she said later, "I suddenly found myself at the head of a family." It was difficult, but with money her father had saved, a small salary she earned from a job teaching in a rural school, and the help of friends and relatives, Ida managed to care for her sisters and brothers for several years until they could take care of themselves.

Later, Ida moved to Chicago and married Ferdinand Barnett, an attorney. They had four children. Ida had become an important writer and crusader for the fair treatment of American blacks, but she was faced with the dilemma of dividing her time between her children and her career. With her husband's support, she chose to devote herself to motherhood and homemaking until her youngest child was in school. Only then did she return to her outside work, always making sure that her youngsters were well cared for after school hours.

The Wellses and Barnetts, and indeed most people of that era, believed that the American family was the heart of society and that the nation's future depended on its strength. Certainly, many ills befell the family—untimely deaths, financial struggles, misunderstandings between immigrant parents and their children, separation of family members—but despite such troubles, family ties remained firm.

Modern Times

As the century drew to a close, more and more people were becoming educated, marrying at a later age, and having smaller families. Moral attitudes were strong, and the upbringing of children for the most part was strict. Increasingly, American families were living in modern homes with electricity and new time- and labor-saving conveniences like toasters, irons, vacuum cleaners, and washing and sewing machines. Some homes even included a plumbing system. A telephone in the home was still rare, but by fifteen years later it was common for people to ring the operator and be connected to someone at the other end of the line elsewhere in town. With all of these conveniences and with fewer children to look after, women were freer to join gardening or literary clubs, lend a helping hand in hospitals or orphanages, and work outside the home in offices, libraries, or stores.

People who had no special knowledge of camera technique could use a new wonder developed by George Eastman at his Kodak company—a hand-held camera. The film was easy to load, and with

*Advertisement for men's
work clothing*
Levi Strauss & Company,
San Francisco

only a simple button to press—click!—like magic anyone could take a photograph of a family picnic in the park, a school graduation, or a holiday gathering. In 1900, Eastman introduced another camera, one especially for children. It was called the Brownie, and it sold for a dollar.

In the cities, department stores offered almost all kinds of merchandise under one roof. Specialty chain stores, like the F. W. Woolworth Company, were also growing in number. At Woolworth, customers could buy lipstick, ribbon, thread, gum drops, chewing gum, or Valentine candy hearts bearing the message, "I Love You Truly." At a tobacconist's, with the purchase of a pack of cigarettes, customers could get a picture of a stage actress, or of a baseball player from a team like the Cincinnati Red Stockings or the Louisville Grays.

Coca Cola ad
Courtesy of the Archives,
the Coca Cola Company

The drugstore was a favorite place to visit. At Loeb & Hollis in Junction City, Kansas, a customer could buy perfume, a cigar, or cough syrup. A school girl or boy was more likely to sit at the soda fountain and sip a lemon phosphate for a nickel or an ice cream soda for a dime. The family could dine out at Frey's Cafe nearby on Main Street. A dinner of navy bean soup, roast beef, mashed potatoes, and rhubarb pie added up to a bill of forty cents.

In rural areas, home shoppers could fill their needs through the mail-order catalogs, which became known as wish books. Montgomery Ward and Sears, Roebuck companies offered thousands of items. Through the catalogs, customers could purchase a baby buggy, a porcelain dinner set, fleece-lined underwear, a pair of high

Page from an 1898 Sears, Roebuck catalog. Millions of rural citizens shopped by mail order from catalogs that were called wish books.
Sears, Roebuck, and Company

button shoes, a set of tools, a colored glass lamp—even a tractor or a piano!

Many books and pamphlets urged homemakers everywhere to keep well-ordered homes. Women also sought advice from a man named Edward Bok, editor of one of the most popular magazines of the day, the *Ladies' Home Journal.* Bok, a self-educated Dutch immigrant, became a journalist after working his way up from a job as Western Union office boy. He printed columns of advice on topics ranging from affairs of the heart, etiquette, beauty hints, and medical do's and don'ts to the best methods of flower and furniture arranging. He freely offered his opinions: "This chair is ugly," or "This table is beautiful." He also opined that he did not like lipstick, bobbed hair, short stockings, or a girl going out with a young man unchaperoned.

Gibson Girl, as drawn by
Charles Dana Gibson
Dover Publications, Inc.

Dream Girl

The most popular girl in the nation was the Gibson Girl. She was the creation of magazine illustrator Charles Dana Gibson. She was charming, gracious, fascinating, polite, inquisitive, modest, willing to learn, and possessed a fine beauty. She was the "typical, true American girl." She captivated men and inspired women, who imitated her looks and the way they thought she behaved. Little girls adorned their rooms with her picture, bought pillowcases and souvenir spoons bearing her replica, and dreamed of growing up to be like her. Early drawings showed her wearing a puffy-sleeved shirtwaist and an ankle-length skirt, with a pompadour crow's nest hairstyle—the crowning glory of 1890s fashions—topped off by a smart straw hat. In time, she reflected women's increasing activities outside the home. She appeared in turn flirtatious or sentimental, athletic or ambitious. She even appeared as a college graduate in cap and gown, about to face "old man world." There was a Gibson man, too, well groomed, square shouldered, and clean shaven, which started to put men's mustaches out of fashion.

The New Woman

Women were making strides in many areas, but they still had a long way to go to achieve respect, freedom, and equality. Many people, men and women alike, frowned upon women's new, more active role in society, while others angrily attacked it. Thinkers sympathetic to women's rights also spoke out; sometimes, however, they couldn't practice their beliefs in their own lives. Frederic Howe, a writer and reformer, had long believed in equality for women, but when he married Marie Jenney, a Unitarian minister, suddenly he didn't want her to work anymore. "I wanted my old-fashioned picture of a wife rather than equal partner," he admitted, describing an image that many men held: "Men and women fell in love, they married, had children; the wife cooked the meals, kept the house clean, entertained friends . . . cared for the family when sick, got the children ready for school and church, arranged the men's clothes . . . made cakes and pies for the church sociables . . . She was careful of her conduct, and only had an opinion of her own in a whisper."

Women were a growing part of the work force, although they were paid considerably less than men. They were bicycling and playing tennis, which allowed them to step out of their long, billowy skirts and bustles and show a bit of stockinged leg, but they were still laced into tight corsets. (A Trenton, New Jersey, store ran a daring ad for a skirt "short enough to avoid entanglement with skates.") Women joined clubs to expand their interests, although sometimes when they did they were called social butterflies.

Suffragists had been working to win the women's vote with little success ever since the goal had been announced at a women's convention in Seneca Falls, New York, in 1848. (The territories of Wyoming and Utah and the states of Colorado and Idaho, where women worked alongside men, gave females the vote in the mid-1800s. The struggle for a national law went on so long that most of the suffrage leaders, such as Elizabeth Cady Stanton, Susan B. Anthony, Sojourner Truth, Lucretia Mott, Lucy Stone, and the Reverend Anna Howard Shaw, never lived to see the goal achieved. That was because the Nineteenth Amendment to the U.S. Constitution, which granted American women the right to vote, was not passed until 1920—seventy-two years after the battle had begun!

School Days

Americans believed that education would ensure a nation of continued democratic principles and actions. But free education for everyone was a complex process that involved making changes and improvements.

Around 1900, more than 16 million pupils were enrolled in elementary and secondary schools. Junior highs were a new innovation, and adult evening schools were on the rise. Several hundred colleges existed, including a number of women's schools. Many universities, which had formerly admitted only men, were opening their doors to women as well. New colleges specializing in programs such as business, teaching, and the fine arts also opened up.

Throughout the century, schoolwork had consisted mostly of reading, writing, and a bit of calculation. Most lessons were taught by rote memory. The basic schoolbooks for the previous decades had been the McGuffey *Readers*, which were full of moral stories followed by vocabulary lists. One story told about a boy named John Jones, who

didn't play until his work was done because he knew that it was "bad for us not to work." Another told of a girl who was always truthful, however, "shame, shame on the child who cannot be believed and who is regarded with suspicion."

By the 1890s, many schools offered more varied and less rigid instruction, and pupils could study additional subjects such as science, art, music, and physical education. A new educational philosophy was put forth by John Dewey, a university professor. Dewey believed that early environment and home training played an important part in a child's success or failure in school. Dewey also felt that lessons learned from books weren't enough; school must also relate to personal experience and expression. These were startling new ideas and prompted numerous lengthy debates among educators.

In Charleston, South Carolina, young Mamie Garvin had a cousin called Lala, a schoolteacher, who introduced the child to spelling, arithmetic, and geography. Then Mamie enrolled in a black elementary school across town, where she became a prize pupil. She was eager to continue her education at the high school level, but there were no public high schools for black children, and her family could not afford to send her to a private institution. Fortunately, Mamie received a scholarship to a black school in another town. There she majored in pedagogy, a program that combined learning to become a teacher with classwork in English, history, math, science, music, and Bible studies. The daily routine was rigid, requiring everyone to rise at 5:00 A.M., clean their rooms, dress, and attend devotions in chapel before beginning classroom work. With neither running water nor electricity, pupils had to haul water and study by kerosene lamp. School life for Mamie and her classmates was rigorous indeed, but Mamie was ever grateful for the opportunity to learn. Later Mamie Garvin became a teacher like her beloved cousin, Lala.

The Pleasures of Reading

Once, libraries had been small rooms for the cultural pursuits of a select few. But with the rise of education, a need for more libraries also arose. Steel magnate Andrew Carnegie, a lover of books, gave financial gifts to more than seventeen hundred American cities to build libraries. Soon, an abundance of books and periodicals became available to an eager public. Readers in Dallas, Texas, had been using a room in a building on Main Street. When they saw the completion of a new Carnegie library in nearby Fort Worth, they formed a library association and wrote to the Carnegie foundation, suggesting that Dallas, with a population of fifty thousand, would be a good place for another one. Mr. Carnegie agreed. According to his policy, he promised to

Checkout desk at the Dallas Public Library
Texas/Dallas History and Archives, Dallas Public Library

give a large donation, but only on the condition that the town pledge to continue to support the facility. Fund-raising got under way at once. Soon, Dallas had erected a two-story public library for its enthusiastic patrons.

In Independence, Missouri, the town library was situated next to the high school, making it especially convenient for students to study or browse. Two frequent visitors were childhood pals, Charlie Ross and Harry Truman. Harry, who later became a U.S. president (and chose Charlie as his press secretary), was a devoted reader of history books and biographies of military heroes; for him, he later said, this reading was not just "romantic adventure," but "solid instruction and wise teaching." It was not surprising, then, that in school he excelled in history. Harry Truman would always acknowledge his debt to his teachers and the town librarian, Carrie Wallace, for their guidance in his education.

In Washington, D.C., in 1900, the Library of Congress, near the U.S. Capitol, boasted of having catalogued more than a million books and other items of reading material to serve the nation.

During this period, the literary tastes of the American people were changing. Before the end of the century, the most frequently read novels in America were those by British authors like Charles Dickens, Rudyard Kipling, and Robert Louis Stevenson. Their books were easily reprinted in America because no international copyright law prevented publishers from doing so. But such a copyright act was enacted in 1891, which put a stop to reprinting books from abroad at will. Now, legal permission to do so was needed. It was a good time for more Americans to be encouraged to write literature and more sophisticated works than the popular action, adventure, and romance stories that writers were churning out.

A new national literary spirit was born—and with it a style of literary realism and naturalism that reflected the way people really lived, including their tragedies and their struggles to survive. One of the most popular American writers was Mark Twain, a master of folk literature and author of the beloved novels *The Adventures of Tom Sawyer* and *The Adventures of Huckleberry Finn*. Twain (1835-1910) was born Samuel Langhorne Clemens and grew up in Hannibal, Missouri, where he lived firsthand many of the adventures he wrote about. The Clemens family was poor, and after the death of his father, eleven-year-old Samuel quit school (which he had little heart for anyway) and went to work learning the printing trade. But the lad, who became self-educated, was never one to stay in any place for long.

Early in his career, he embarked upon a boat trip from New Orleans down to the Amazon River in South America. But once he was on a steamer, he got caught up in the thrill and challenge of river-

Mark Twain
Mark Twain Memorial,
Hartford, Connecticut

boating. He postponed his planned trip and instead remained several years as a pilot on the Mississippi River. It was from those days that Clemens took his pen name, Mark Twain, a riverboat term meaning water "two fathoms deep," a safe depth for navigation.

Twain spent his life traveling the world and writing about his observations and experiences in books, newspapers, and magazines. His serious writings were well received, but he was most popular for his thoughtful humor and satire of society's pompous and hypocritical members of the Gilded Age, the phrase that he had created.

Other renowned authors of the time were Stephen Crane, who wrote *The Red Badge of Courage*, a masterpiece about the Civil War; Henry James, whose novels compared the innocence of Americans to the more sophisticated and worldly Europeans; Hamlin Garland, who realistically described prairie life, which he both loved and hated; and Joel Chandler Harris of Georgia, author of the Uncle Remus stories, traditional black tales that became an important contribution to American folklore.

Literature for young readers consisted mostly of the moral tale, in which the character was rewarded for virtuous behavior. *Little Lord Fauntleroy*, a story about a young English lord, and *Five Little Peppers and How They Grew*, a loving family story, were widely read. For decades, a favorite girls' book was *Little Women* by Louisa May Alcott. Louisa May's own family life did not bring her much happiness; her father failed to give her affection, and his inability to make an adequate living forced Louisa May to support the Alcotts with earnings from her published stories. In *Little Women*, Alcott portrayed an idealized home life she yearned to have.

Boys' stories of danger and death-defying adventures became the rage. They were called dime novels and were often forbidden by parents. One fellow recalled, "I read them at every chance; so did every normal boy. We traded lesser treasures for them; we swapped them on the basis of two old volumes for one new one; . . . the more daring among us read them in school behind the shelter of an open geography propped up on the desk." Once, that same fellow was caught in the act of reading a dime novel at home, and for his disobedience he was given a sound paddling.

Changes in journalism in the 1890s included not only increasing newspaper circulation but a new sensational style of writing and publishing. No longer was news written in a matter-of-fact style with the same size lettering in small columns of type. Now, bold headlines of death, accidents, gossip, even impending war, as well as big front-page photographs, screamed out to capture the buying public. Two

The Neely family enjoyed an evening together, making music and popping corn in the parlor of their Florence, Oregon home.
Lane County Historical Museum, Eugene, Oregon

publishers competing for readership were responsible for sensational journalism: Joseph Pulitzer, publisher of the *St. Louis Post-Dispatch* and the *New York World*, and William Randolph Hearst, owner of the *New York Journal*. Pulitzer was the first to run a cartoon character—a funny-looking ragamuffin kid with big ears and a baggy yellow shirt. He was called the Yellow Kid, and from 1896 on, newspaper sensationalism became known as "yellow journalism."

Music and Art

People enjoyed sentimental songs from all regions of the country: "My Old Kentucky Home," "The Sidewalks of New York," "On the Banks of the Wabash, Far Away." They sang and played hit tunes like

"A Hot Time in the Old Town Tonight," "My Wild Irish Rose," and "Daisy Bell" ("A Bicycle Built for Two"). They marched to snappy band music like "The Stars and Stripes Forever," composed by John Philip Sousa, leader of the U.S. Marine Band for many years. In the larger cities, they attended grand opera and classical music performances by newly organized symphony orchestras, which played works of the great European composers.

But what could America, in its comparatively short history, claim as its own original and authentic music? What captured the American spirit? It was black folk music, originating from what was once called the Negro spiritual—the deeply felt, soulful music of southern slaves. This music was the most spontaneous, earthy, and moving form of musical expression, as well as the most genuine and enduring. Many songs grew out of that spirit, like "Carry Me Back to Old Virginny" and "In the Evening by the Moonlight," and were soon featured in musical theater and minstrel shows. The syncopated melody of ragtime, created especially for piano, also emerged. Its most representative piece was "Maple Leaf Rag" by Scott Joplin, a Texas musician.

American art, too, was beginning to come into its own. Like novelists of the time, artists and sculptors turned away from an earlier style of romanticism to express realism on canvas and in sculpture. Of the painters who emerged, two of the most acclaimed were Winslow Homer and Frederic Remington. Homer, who settled in a remote region on the coast of Maine, was most noted for his intense, stirring paintings of the sea and the rugged men who followed sea life. Remington, who left his upstate New York home for the West, realized there that the "vacant land and the wild riders were about to vanish forever." He began to sketch, sculpt (mostly in bronze), and paint the legendary life he saw around him—the cowboy at the watering hole, the American Indian scouting for friends, the prairie pony, the cavalry soldier, and the landscapes of the last frontier. Remington became the true historian of the Old West.

Amusements and Recreation

Theater provided amusement—song and dance acts of vaudeville and musical comedy—as well as serious drama in productions such as Shakespearean history or tragedy. The play *Uncle Tom's Cabin*, adapted from Harriet Beecher Stowe's powerful and provocative antislavery novel of 1852, was still so popular long after the Civil War that in 1900 it was the biggest money maker on the New York stage. Other kinds of amusement were the light-opera house, the traveling Buffalo Bill Wild West Show, or a vacation at the shore. City folks could catch a trolley out to an amusement park, ride the merry-go-round, dance in the pavilion, and win a prize at the shooting gallery.

And for many a rural lad or lass there was the magic of the circus. In Oregon, one boy found that "the lure of sawdust and spangles was much stronger than family ties or the red schoolhouse," so he ran away to join the Mighty Yankee Robinson Circus, where he was hired as a block boy to help set up and tear down the seats. But after four days of experiencing the thrill of life with circus folks, he was dragged home and given a licking and a stern lecture. Back at school, he was considered a hero by his friends. He knew that some-day he would become a showman, and later he joined a circus and worked under the big top for sixty years.

Nothing caught the nation's fancy quite like the bicycle. In 1896, there were 4 million bicycle riders—on two-wheelers, three-wheelers (for ladies not daring enough to wear bloomers), and bicycles built for two. Cycling was considered good exercise and a sport fit for the entire family. Sports such as football and boxing were growing in popularity, especially in the eastern colleges, and golf and tennis were favorite games of the wealthy. But the sport that swept the country was the all-American game of baseball. Everyone had a favorite hero and a favorite team. "Baseball," Mark Twain said, "is the very symbol, the outward and visible expression of the drive and push and rush and struggle of the raging, tearing, booming nineteenth century."

10

Way Out West

Out on the Plains there lived a pioneer named Mary Elizabeth Lease. People called her by other names, too, depending on how they felt about her. Folks who liked Mrs. Lease and viewed her as an admired leader in their fight for their fair economic share in society called her "Our Queen Mary." Those who opposed her political views, or disliked a woman who spoke her mind and expressed her opinions freely, called her "the Kansas Pythoness." Newspapermen who saw both sides described her as "un-American," "a lantern-jawed, eagle-eyed nightmare," or "raw-boned and ugly as a mud hen." But they also admitted that Mrs. Lease was a fiery and dynamic speaker who could draw a crowd of thousands and keep them spellbound for hours.

Lease, the mother of four (two children died in infancy), was a stately, gaunt woman, nearly six feet tall, who often wore a black dress with a brooch pinned at the neck. She had come from a Pennsylvania farming town, had graduated from a teaching academy at fifteen, and had packed up and moved to the Plains in the hope of earning a

Mary Elizabeth Lease

THE DISTINGUISHED
AUTHOR AND LECTURER.

A high-styled advertisement for a speaking engagement by Mary Lease, who traveled widely and urged farmers to demand their rights
The Kansas State Historical Society, Topeka, Kansas

decent wage as a schoolteacher. After teaching in a Catholic girls' school for a while, she married a druggist who couldn't always find work. The couple tried farming in various places before settling in Wichita, Kansas, where Mary managed to study law and be admitted to the district bar of Wichita. Wherever she lived she found herself involved in women's and political organizations. She grew steadily as a professional lecturer, stirring her audiences for the causes of women's rights, workers' rights, and finally farmers' rights.

But she gained her greatest stature and fame as a champion of the discontented farmers and their plight. The rich were getting

By the 1890s, most prairie families lived in log cabins, but many, like this family near McCook, Nebraska, still dwelled in homes dug out of the earth.
Nebraska State Historical Society

richer, and the poor were getting poorer. The farmers—providers of the nation—were not acquiring any of the riches that the powerful, eastern industrialists were enjoying.

In fact, the farmers of the West and the South felt so betrayed by the eastern industrial monopolies and the federal government that they were gathering their forces for revolt. They believed that big business was crushing them—especially the railroad companies, who could charge as much as they wanted to transport the farmers' produce, and banks and loan companies, which kept raising their interest rates, making it more difficult to borrow money for necessary farm

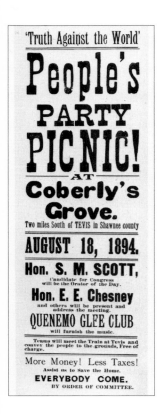

equipment. Every year, farmers were falling deeper into debt. A series of droughts, waves of economic depression, and a continual drop in the price of staple crops like wheat, corn, and cotton set them back still further. Moreover, the era of settling the frontier's "free land" had come to an end.

The farmers were so desperate and angry that they became an eager audience for a woman like Mary Elizabeth Lease, who had always sympathized with the oppressed and the exploited. On the lecture stump, she cried out to the crowds, "It is no longer a government of the people, by the people, and for the people—but a government of Wall Street, by Wall Street, and for Wall Street. The great common people of this country are slaves, and monopoly is the master." The crowds cheered wildly when she whipped them up with her rallying cry of "raise less corn and more hell."

And so the people rallied. Led by Lease and other passionate orators like Ignatius Donnelly, reformer, journalist, and eccentric personality, and Jeremiah "Sockless" Simpson, a Kansas congressman, the farmers joined already established agricultural alliances and some labor groups to organize a third party.

The party was called the People's Party, but it became known as the Populists, and it stood for reforms to help and protect farmers and laborers. Its first national convention was held in 1892 in Omaha, Nebraska. Ignatius Donnelly wrote a bold preamble to the platform. "We meet in the midst of a nation brought to the verge of moral, political, and material ruin. Corruption dominates the ballot-box. . . . The people are demoralized . . . our homes covered with mortgages; labor impoverished and the land concentrated in the hands of the capitalists."

The Populists called for an increase in the amount of money in circulation by allowing unlimited coinage of silver to supplement gold as the standard of money. An increase of money would cause prices to rise—inflation—which would benefit the farmers, who were debtors because they had to borrow from banks and creditors every year to

William Jennings Bryan
Library of Congress

keep their farms operating. The Populists further demanded public ownership of the railroads and telegraph and telephone systems; a graduated income tax; and government-operated postal savings banks to guarantee money deposits. They also favored the eight-hour workday and immigration restriction.

The new party nominated James Weaver of Iowa as their presidential candidate. He turned out to be an unfortunate choice, however. He was unknown in many parts, and he preached such different political and economic ideas from the mainstream that many considered him extreme, or radical. Weaver and the Republican candidate lost to the Democratic nominee, Grover Cleveland, in Cleveland's second bid for the White House. Despite the Populists' national loss, they won statewide gains, and their campaign made an impact on the American political scene.

In Nebraska, another reformer and silver-tongued speaker also rose to prominence around the same time as the Populist leaders—

William Jennings Bryan. As a child, he had learned to read early, and after memorizing long passages, he stood on top of a table and recited them to his mother. When he was twelve, his father took him to a Democratic rally in their hometown of Salem, Illinois, and at the end Bryan mounted the platform and proceeded to discuss a current issue. At first, the men in the audience laughed at the boy orator, but he kept on talking until they began to listen, and, finally, they cheered him on. In school, Bryan won oratory contests as well as essay competitions, and at his college graduation he delivered the valedictory speech. He went on to study law and eventually moved to Lincoln, Nebraska. In time, he was elected to Congress as a Democrat but later lost a bid for the Senate. Back then, senators were chosen by state legislators, rather than by direct popular vote.

Populist leader Bryan championed the hard-working farmers, and he traveled widely on their behalf. When his wife once asked him to stop traveling so much, he replied, "I must continue to fight the battles of the people, for what I think is right and just." Since the Democrats favored most Populist issues, they also favored Bryan as their presidential candidate. At the 1896 convention, the Populists merged with the Democratic party, and Bryan's name was placed on the ballot.

The election, a fierce struggle between the common people and the rich, was the most bitter the country had ever known. The Populist governor of Kansas referred to the eastern powers as "the plutocrats, the aristocrats, and all the other rats." The battle between gold and silver advocates over the monetary standard became the foremost campaign issue. The great amount of gold found earlier during the California and Nevada gold rush had declined by the early 1890s, and the U.S. gold treasury was drained. Silver was becoming easier to process and was gaining in value. The Populists wanted free, unlimited coinage of silver to increase the supply—and also to wrest power from the very rich. Bryan strongly promoted the silver movement. At the Democratic national convention in Chicago, he delivered

William McKinley
Library of Congress

what was considered the most famous oration since Lincoln's Gettysburg Address—the "Cross of Gold" speech. In brilliant oratorical style, Bryan answered the Republican party's demand for the gold standard with a great burst of discourse. He ended dramatically, "You shall not press down upon the brow of labor this crown of thorns, you shall not crucify mankind upon a cross of gold."

When he finished his speech he sat down to stunned silence. But the audience quickly recovered, and for an hour afterward the twenty thousand delegates shouted, stomped, and rejoiced in their new leader. One writer said that Bryan "had found magic words for the feeling" that the people had been unable to express. "He had played at their very heart-strings, until the full tide of their emotion was let loose in one tempestuous roar of passion."

Bryan traveled thousands of miles across twenty-one states throughout the campaign. The Populists put up a courageous fight, but in the end they lost. The winner was William McKinley, an Ohio Republican who had a well-organized and especially well-funded campaign, though he hardly left his front porch in Canton, because of his invalid wife. Nor did McKinley offer a strong platform. He chose not to take a stand on most issues, although it was known that he stood for gold.

Complicated social and economic changes had determined the outcome of the election, and it was not easy to figure out exactly why the Populists and Democrats were defeated or why Populism lost its strength so quickly afterward. Historians have offered many reasons: One was that Americans were reluctant to change allegiance from traditional party ideals. Another was that Easterners opposed the movement as too radical. Perhaps one of the strongest reasons is that by the end of 1896 national prosperity was beginning to return. Silver started dropping, and crop production and prices were rising. People saw less need for "revolutionary" solutions to economic ills.

Meanwhile, rumors poured in from the Yukon River region, an American territory far to the north. Gold! Gold had been discovered, and thousands of frenzied prospectors, buckskin bags on their backs, rushed to northwestern Canada and the new frontier of Alaska. Only a few prospectors were successful at getting rich quick. All had to struggle with the treacherous climate and steep, icy, snow-covered slopes; some died in an avalanche that buried them on the famous Chilkoot Pass. Then gold was also found in Australia and South Africa. By 1898, 22 million dollars' worth of gold had been mined and brought into U.S. circulation to help the nation's recovering economy. In 1900, Congress passed an act making gold the single standard of U.S. currency.

Even though the battle over the monetary standard was finally settled and the nation was experiencing prosperity once again, the scorn that Westerners and Easterners felt toward each other remained. To Westerners, the people of the eastern states were mostly city slickers in fancy clothes, rich snobs, and Wall Street dandies, who were all too powerful. To Easterners, the West was primarily an untamed wilderness, populated by rugged cowboys, "savage Indians,"

*Cowboys branding cattle
on the Garst Ranch, near
Coldwater, Kansas*
The Kansas State
Historical Society, Topeka,
Kansas

wise-talking saloon hall women, and outlaws and gunslingers like the notorious Billy the Kid and Jesse James. These exaggerated views of western adventure and romance inspired popular stories and were later perpetuated in Hollywood movies. In time, though, historians would remind us of harsh realities in the West, too, like the rigors of living and working on the cattle range, the shameful treatment of native peoples, and the plundering of the environment. Given both the romance and the realities, the settlers of the West a century ago played a remarkable role in American life, helping to give the nation its earthiness, inventiveness, and imagination.

11

America Becomes a World Power

$\mathbf{A}$t the end of the 1890s, America was about to enter a completely new era. So far, the country had put all its energies into its birth as a self-governing democracy and then into developing its vast resources, while remaining an isolated nation. Now, for the first time, America was looking beyond its national borders toward involvement in international affairs.

One person who was keenly aware of these coming changes was Theodore Roosevelt. In the spring of 1897, he left his position as New York City police commissioner to become assistant secretary of the U.S. Navy. He came to the job eagerly because he understood that the navy would play a foremost role as America made its way onto the world stage. Also, Roosevelt had long been fascinated with naval war. Influenced by an important book—the work of an American admiral—that promoted naval preparedness, Roosevelt had also written a book on sea power, expressing his belief that diplomacy was useless without force behind it. Besides, that spring Roosevelt felt certain that

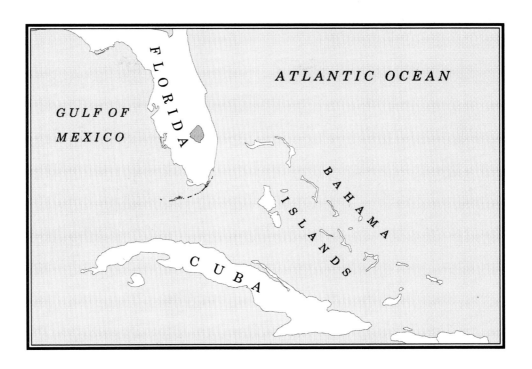

the U.S. was actually headed for war, and he wanted to be assured of victory.

The trouble spot was on the island of Cuba, which was ruled by Spain. Spanish rule had become increasingly tyrannical. When Cuban rebels began fighting for freedom and independence, Spain cruelly responded by killing the insurgents or forcing them into concentration camps. America sympathized with the plight of the Cubans and viewed itself as liberator of the island.

Besides hoping to free Cuba, the U.S. also wanted to expand its economic and political interests to foreign shores. America had invested much money in Cuba's tobacco and sugar industries, because it was a rich island that could yield good profits for American business concerns. Also, American industrial output had grown so enormously and its natural resources had become so plentiful that the country needed new foreign markets to which it could sell its surplus goods. In the Far East, for example, European countries, as well as Japan, were already deeply engaged in trade with China. The U.S. realized that it must compete before other countries took control of all Far Eastern trade. At the same time, America recognized that only by establishing military defensive outposts could the nation protect itself. The country, then, needed to find a way to acquire such outposts.

In his Washington, D.C., office, Roosevelt took an active role from the start. He insisted that he "abhorred unjust war," but he was so convinced that war with Spain was just and inevitable, as well as "advantageous to the honor and the interests of the nation," that he arranged for a larger naval buildup.

By the following February, riots in Cuba had worsened to the point that President McKinley dispatched a U.S. battleship, the *Maine*, to the harbor in Havana to keep watch and protect Americans and their property. On the night of February 15, 1898, the *Maine* was rocking gently in its mooring. Some of the crew of 354 had gone to sleep, and others were patrolling the deck. The bugler blew taps, and all was well. Suddenly at 9:40 P. M., with no warning, a tremendous explosion ripped through the ship. The fiery blast hurled metal fragments in every direction, the air grew thick with smoke, water rushed through the torn hull. The screams of the injured could be heard everywhere. Survivors clambered into lifeboats. Within minutes the *Maine*, a mass of twisted wreckage, sank into the sea. In all, 266 men died in the blast or drowned. It was indeed a tragedy; moreover, it finally triggered the anticipated war.

There was never any proof that Spain had blown up the ship, and the cause of the blast remains a mystery, but Americans refused to listen to reports suggesting possible accidental causes. Instead, they accused Spain of committing an act of aggression. The war cry was "Remember the *Maine!*"

The public was further whipped into frenzy by the Hearst and Pulitzer newspapers in their own battle for more readers. Each tried to outdo the other with blaring headlines nearly begging for war. William Randolph Hearst was so bent on going to war that early on he hired the artist Frederic Remington and sent him to Cuba to sketch

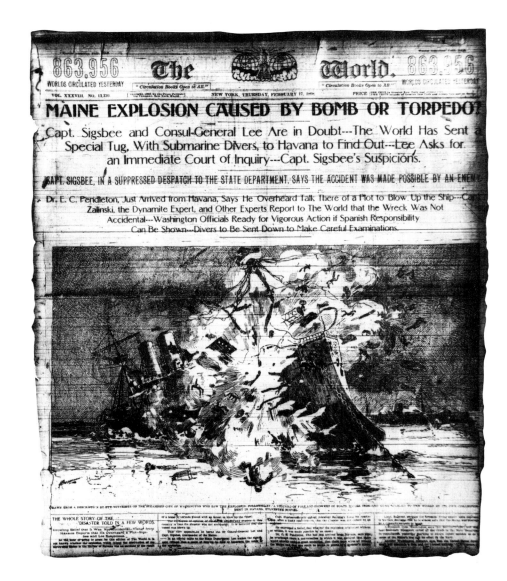

scenes of rebels fighting for their freedom. When Remington arrived, he found little happening. He telegraphed Hearst, "Everything quiet, no trouble here. There will be no war. I wish to return." Hearst replied, "Please remain. You furnish the pictures and I will furnish the war."

President McKinley hoped to find a peaceful solution to the crisis, but that was not to happen. On April 25, 1898, the U.S. officially declared war against Spain. The war was fought both on land and at

Charge of the Rough Riders at San Juan Hill *was painted by Frederic Remington in 1898. Theodore Roosevelt took charge of the volunteer cavalry in Cuba when America declared war on Spain to liberate Cubans from Spanish rule.* Frederic Remington Art Museum, Ogdensburg, New York

sea. Although the American navy was not as well prepared as Roosevelt had hoped it would be, the Spanish navy was even less ready; within days America scored easy victories in both Havana Harbor and in the Far East in a bay off the Philippine Islands, which were also ruled by Spain. U.S. troops landed on the island of Cuba and fought valiantly into the summer before emerging victorious.

Roosevelt, once a boxing champion, a big game hunter, and a rancher in the North Dakota badlands, insisted on joining the battle.

As soon as the war began, he left Washington and helped form the First U.S. Volunteer Cavalry, which was made up of recruits ranging from cowboys and mining prospectors to football players and eastern college graduates. There were black men, white men, and Native Americans as well; all fought side by side. The cavalry became famous as the Rough Riders, and Roosevelt returned home a hero.

In August of 1898, Spain surrendered. One statesman called it "a splendid little war." Roosevelt said, "It was not much of a war but the only one we had." Remarkably few American lives—289—were lost in battle, but, ironically, thousands of soldiers fell ill and died from typhoid, dysentery, spoiled meat, and the diseases of the tropics: malaria and yellow fever.

With the signing of the peace treaty, the U.S. had not only freed Cuba from Spanish control and gained a stratetgic outpost, but also acquired the Philippine Islands, the island of Guam, and Porto Rico (the spelling was later changed to Puerto Rico). America had plunged into war and basked in success afterward, but suddenly it found itself in a new position and was uncertain about what to do with its newly acquired territories. These territories included Hawaii, which had been annexed in a separate action. Questions plagued the government and the people: Should Cuba be allowed to govern itself? Should the Philippines be given independence? If not, how should they be governed? How much should the U.S. be involved in the control of foreign land and in arranging protective outposts and bases for trading, especially in China? Would the navy need to expand in order to protect the colonies? Should a canal be built at the Panama isthmus to create a shorter route between the Atlantic and Pacific oceans? Would heavy foreign entanglement lead to more wars?

These were problems and issues that America hadn't foreseen, and they divided the country into two camps: those who wanted their nation to be a colonial power (possessing colonies) and who especially wanted to keep the Philippine Islands to assure American destiny in the Pacific; and those who opposed such imperialist expansion,

believing it immoral and ruinous to the nation's "fundamental principles and noblest ideals." After all, only a little more than a century had passed since America had fought and won her own independence. President McKinley, a mild-mannered man, had a hard time making up his mind; finally he decided to keep the islands, and the Senate narrowly voted in agreement. The U.S. was now a world power, and the war had been the turning point that brought about this new role.

On January 1, 1900, the new year arrived, marking the momentous dawn of the twentieth century. Despite a multitude of problems facing their modern industrial and colonial nation, Americans entered the new century with a spirit of optimism. They looked forward to a future of growth and prosperity. Now thoroughly intolerant of the wide gap between the rich and the poor, many Americans eagerly supported a progressive movement of social and political reform to improve the public's welfare.

In the presidential election of 1900, McKinley and Bryan once again opposed each other. But this time, President McKinley had a new running mate on the Republican ticket—the popular war hero, Theodore Roosevelt. He had been serving as governor of New York when he was thrust onto the national scene. But he was reluctant to be placed on the ticket, fearing that an insignificant role as vice president would end his political career. In November, McKinley and Roosevelt won by a large margin.

One September day the following year, President McKinley was attending an exhibition in Buffalo, New York. A plain-looking man joined a crowd gathering around the president. Suddenly, the man raised his hand revealing a revolver he had concealed in a handkerchief and fired twice. McKinley lay wounded for a week before he died. The assassin said that he opposed U.S. foreign policy and didn't want so much power put into the hands of one person.

On September 14, 1901, Theodore Roosevelt, statesman, soldier, sportsman, and scholar, took the oath of office as twenty-sixth president of the United States. He was forty-two years old, the youngest president in the country's history. The man who had earlier feared the end of his political career was now the nation's leader.

Theodore Roosevelt was described as a man of "snap and vigor." He brought strength and vitality to the White House. He was strongly principled and insisted upon honesty at all levels of government and business. He aimed to give all Americans a "square deal." Of course, public figures are always subject to criticism, and Roosevelt was no exception. He angered some and quarreled with others. But he remained a man of firm and decisive action.

In foreign policy, Roosevelt spoke of neither imperialism nor expansionism, but of acting in accord with humanitarian ideals toward America's new colonies. He believed in diplomacy and negotiation between governments to avoid unjust wars. But he also believed in maintaining a strong military, and he oversaw a continual buildup of army and navy forces. With his secretary of state, he worked to keep open and fair trade for all countries with China. Furthermore, Roosevelt spearheaded America's construction of a canal in Central America across Panama's isthmus to create a trade route between the Atlantic and Pacific oceans. The project was called "the greatest engineering feat of the age." Roosevelt visited Panama to watch its progress, becoming the first president to leave the country during office.

At home, Roosevelt investigated and regulated big business by urging Congress to establish departments specifically for those purposes and by enforcing the Sherman Antitrust Act. Now the federal government sued corporations for illegal and unethical dealings, which eventually broke the reign of the giant trusts. The public called the president a "trust buster." In the area of labor, Roosevelt considered himself a friend of the working man, but in labor disputes he also favored diplomatic bargaining. When tens of thousands of miners in Pennsylvania's anthracite coal regions went on strike, Roosevelt stepped in to help negotiate a wage settlement between the mine owners and the miners. This was the first time a president played a role in a labor dispute; moreover, his action recognized the existence and the power of unions. In regard to environmental matters, Roosevelt was the first executive to recognize that the country's "natural resources are not inexhaustible"; he created a conservation policy to preserve and reclaim water sources and to set aside millions of acres for national forests.

Encouraged by the president's spirited and vigorous leadership, Americans everywhere strove to bring about political, social, and environmental reforms. One governor and his state inspired other states across the nation. Led by Robert La Follette ("Battling Bob"),

President Theodore Roosevelt confidently helped to shape a new role for the United States.
Library of Congress

Wisconsin was the first to adopt direct primary nomination of political candidates by the people; previously, public officials had chosen candidates behind closed doors. La Follette further urged the regulation of railway rates, a program for compensating workers injured on the job, and a system of fair taxation. People called these measures the "Wisconsin Idea," and they became the backbone of America's progressive movement.

A journalist named Ida M. Tarbell investigated Rockefeller's Standard Oil Company and wrote a series for *McClure's* magazine, in which she exposed in detail the company's vast network of illegal practices. At first, Rockefeller tried to ignore the articles, but his anger soon rose to such a pitch that he started calling Tarbell "Miss Tar Barrel." Tarbell's exposé helped the government prosecute Standard Oil and also helped speed the passage of a bill to establish the two regulatory agencies, the Department of Commerce and the Bureau of Corporations.

Building the Panama Canal in a physically hostile territory was indeed a great engineering feat. But it could not have been accomplished without first conquering another enemy that had destroyed people throughout the ages, especially in tropical regions—yellow fever. Most recently, the disease had killed vast numbers of American soldiers fighting the Spanish in Cuba. It had also killed thousands of Spanish and Cubans. But until the Spanish-American War, there had been no organized attempt to find the cause of the disease. One Cuban doctor had suspected that mosquitoes carried the disease, but few took him seriously. Finally, one man did—Dr. Walter Reed, who headed a U.S. army investigative medical team sent to Cuba. There, Reed and his men undertook a series of trying experiments, in which two team members, as well as several other soldiers, volunteered to be bitten by the suspect, the infected aëdes mosquito. Some of the men died, and others fell ill but recovered. Months later, the doctors had their proof. Following this scientific breakthrough, medical-corps sanitation officers turned efforts toward eradicating the breeding places of mosquito eggs, another difficult task. When they had accomplished this in Cuba, similar actions were taken successfully in Panama. Only then could engineers begin the work of building the canal.

John Muir, an explorer and naturalist, felt a deep appreciation for America's natural beauty and resources; he became an active campaigner for conservation and founded an important conservation organization, the Sierra Club. Muir succeeded in getting Congress to declare California's Yosemite Valley and Sequoia forests as national parks and to establish Arizona's Petrified Forest as a national monument. He also persuaded President Roosevelt to set aside millions of acres of redwood forest for preservation. Because of their mutual concerns, Muir and Roosevelt fostered a steadfast friendship. They even took a camping trip together in Yosemite Valley and hiked in the Sierras, sharing the wonders of their beautiful surroundings.

One summer day, in the middle of a speaking tour, Roosevelt was out riding in a carriage near Pittsfield, Massachusetts. Suddenly, an electric trolley car, traveling too fast, collided with the carriage. A secret service man sitting next to the driver was knocked down and instantly killed. The president and two other men inside the carriage were thrown out onto the road, bruised and shaken, but not seriously injured. Later the president grieved over his attendant's death, but at the moment he got to his feet and cried out, "I am not hurt." Shortly afterward, he insisted on finishing his speaking tour. The president *had* been hurt, however, and later required surgery. But his tough, stouthearted manner and his decisive action were typical of his remarkable character, both as an individual and as a political leader at a crucial time in history.

As the United States moved into the twentieth century, Theodore Roosevelt and the American people were transforming the nation into a dynamic world empire. Many people tried to predict the future. But no one can really predict with accuracy what lies ahead. And certainly, when America stepped onto the world stage, no one could foresee what events would take place and what dramas were to come.

Suggested Reading

Antin, Mary. *The Promised Land.* Boston: Houghton Mifflin, 1911.

Billington, Ray Allen. *Westward Expansion: A History of the American Frontier.* New York: Macmillan, 1960.

Brown, Dee. *Bury My Heart at Wounded Knee, An Indian History of the American West.* New York: Holt, Rinehart and Winston, 1971.

Du Bois, W. E. B. *The Souls of Black Folk.* Chicago: A. C. McClurg & Co., 1903; reissued by Vintage Books, 1990.

Ehrlich, Amy. *Wounded Knee, An Indian History of the American West.* A version of Dee Brown's classic book adapted for young readers. New York: Holt, Rinehart and Winston, 1974.

Fields, Mamie Garvin, written with Karen Fields. *Lemon Swamp and Other Places, A Carolina Memoir.* New York: The Free Press, 1983.

Josephson, Matthew. *Edison, A Biography.* New York: McGraw-Hill, 1959; reissued by John Wiley, 1992.

Lens, Sidney. *Strikemakers and Strikebreakers.* New York: Lodestar Books, 1985.

Marrin, Albert, *The Spanish-American War.* New York: Atheneum, 1991.

McKissack, Patricia and Fred. *A Long, Hard Journey: The Story of the Pullman Porter.* New York: Walker and Co., 1989.

Myers, Walter Dean. *Now Is Your Time! The African-American Struggle for Freedom.* New York: HarperCollins, 1991.

Riis, Jacob A. *How the Other Half Lives.* New York: Scribner's, 1890; reissued by Dover Press, 1971.

Roosevelt, Theodore. *Autobiography.* New York: Scribner's, 1913; reissued by Di Capo/Plenum, 1985.

Serrin, William. *Homestead: The Glory and Tragedy of an American Steel Town.* New York: Times Books, 1992.

Stratton, Joanna L. *Pioneer Women: Voices From the Kansas Frontier.* New York: Touchstone Books/Simon & Schuster, 1981.

Tifft, Wilton S. *Ellis Island.* Chicago: Contemporary Books, 1990.

Washington, Booker T. *Up From Slavery, An Autobiography.* New York: Doubleday, 1901, 1963.

Index

Page numbers in *italics* refer to illustrations and maps.